———

Hoof Care 101:

Hoof Health for Horse Owners

———

Printed in the United States of America

First Printing, 2024

ISBN 979-8-218-32785-9

Sky Island Hoof Care LLC
Bisbee, AZ 85603

www.SkyIslandHoofCare.com

For Patrón:

a horse, who was a very good boy.

HOOFCARE 101 ✚

HOOF HEALTH FOR HORSE OWNERS

ERIK **SERVIA**

ILLUSTRATIONS
BY
KRISTINA **SMITH**

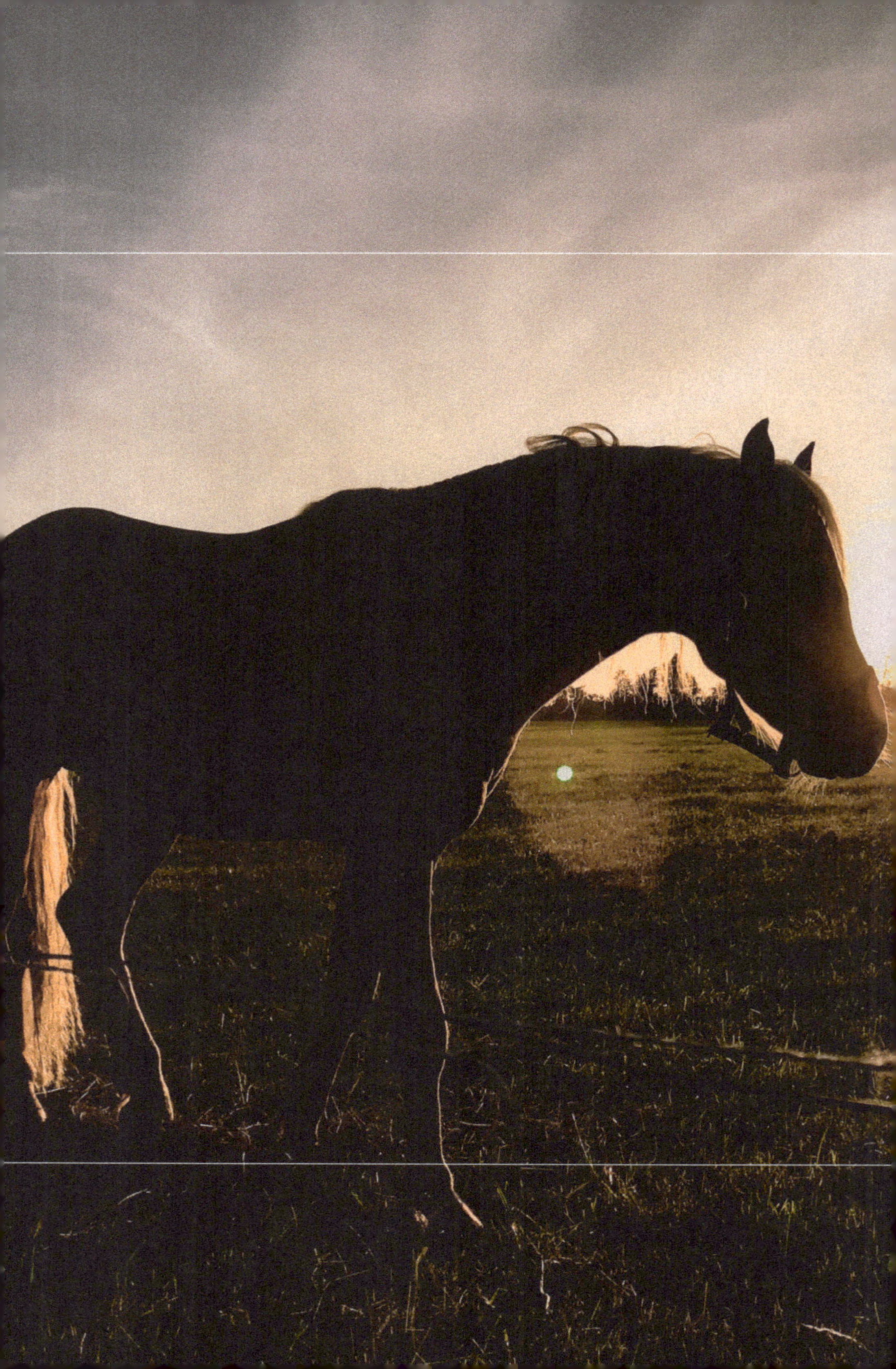

CONTENTS

Introduction

PICASSO WAS A TALL AND GANGLY PAINT HORSE. His hips and spine jutted from his body in all directions, making him look more like an abstract painting of a horse than the real thing. He was found wandering through the desert, dehydrated and starved, emaciated beyond recognition.

The veterinarian estimated Picasso as about 20 years old and concluded he had been suffering from chronic laminitis, which progressed into a more serious founder, for several years. It seemed like the previous owner didn't want to deal with Picasso's ever-increasing vet and farrier bills and special diets. Picasso was set free to fend for himself, in excruciating pain, in the harsh wastelands of Central Arizona.

When I met Picasso, his hooves were about twice as long as they should have been. About a year and a half overdue by my estimation. The chronic founder and poor alignment of bones from lack of trimming had shut-off critical blood supply to his hooves. The coffin bones inside his feet were decaying, creating pockets of necrotic tissue that festered into enormous abscesses that ran the length of his entire sole. He could hardly stand on his own feet.

Picasso was placed into the care of a local rescue where he received many veterinary and farrier check-ups, an easy diet to process with his old teeth and damaged metabolism, and little girls to visit him and brush his mane. He lived several more years.

Picasso's debilitating condition and years of suffering could have been easily prevented. If his owner had provided a simple diet change and regular hoof trimmings, Picasso may still be running and playing today.

Horses have been a part of human history for thousands of years, serving as companions, workers, and even symbols of power and status. The domestication of horses is believed to have occurred around 4000 BC in the steppes of Central Asia, where nomadic tribes began to tame and breed horses for their own use. As society progressed, horses became an essential part of human life, both for transportation and agriculture.

In the modern era, horses have continued to play an important role in human society. Horses are used in various disciplines, such as racing, dressage, jumping, and western riding. Horses are also used in therapy and rehabilitation programs, helping people with physical and emotional challenges. The relationship between humans and horses is unique and complex, shaped by a deep emotional bond that transcends the practical and functional aspects of our interactions with these magnificent animals.

From the moment we lay eyes on them, there is something about their grace, strength, and beauty that draws us in and creates an emotional connection. Horses have a unique way of capturing the hearts of humans, and their care and well-being are crucial to preserving this relationship. Horse owners must take great care of their horses and work closely with farriers, veterinarians, and other professionals to ensure their horses are healthy and happy.

Proper hoof care is essential for the overall well-being of horses, and it is also crucial for maintaining a strong bond between horse and owner. A horse suffering from hoof problems can experience extreme pain, discomfort, and severe lameness. This can lead to a decline in their physical and mental health, which can, in turn, affect their relationship with their owner and other horses. A horse in pain or discomfort is less likely to want to interact with its owner, and its behavior may change, becoming grumpy or hard to handle.

On the other hand, a horse that is well taken care of, with healthy hooves, is a horse that is happy and content. They are more willing to interact with their owners, and their behavior is more predictable. They are less likely to suffer from lameness or other hoof-related problems, making them less likely to need specialized veterinary care. This saves money and ensures that the horse is healthy and happy for a longer period of time.

Proper hoof care is also vital for the horse's and its owner's safety. A horse with healthy hooves is less likely to slip and fall, which can lead to serious injury for everyone involved. It also ensures that the horse can move comfortably and efficiently, which is essential for overall well-being.

In addition to our relationships with horses, regular hoof care also has a practical side. A horse's hooves are absolutely essential for its mobility and health, and it is the owner's responsibility to ensure they are well-maintained. As a horse owner, it is crucial to understand the importance of proper hoof care in maintaining this bond and ensuring the horse's well-being. By staying informed and working closely with a farrier and veterinarian, horse owners can ensure that their horse's hooves are healthy and strong, allowing for a lifetime of enjoyment and companionship.

What is Farriery?

Farriery, the art and science of caring for horses' hooves, has a long and storied history dating back to ancient times.

In ancient civilizations such as Egypt, Greece, and Rome, horses were used for transportation, warfare, and sport. The earliest known depictions of farriery come from ancient Egyptian tomb paintings, which show individuals trimming and dressing horses' hooves.

The first written accounts of hoof care come from the Greeks and Romans, who wrote about the importance of healthy hooves in maintaining the overall health and performance of their horses. The Greek philosopher Xenophon, for example, wrote about the importance of strong hooves in his treatise "On Horsemanship." The Roman author and farmer Columella also wrote about the importance of hoof care in his book "On Agriculture."

"Just as a house would be of little use, however beautiful its upper stories, if the underlying foundations were not what they ought to be, so there is little use to be extracted from a horse, and in particular a war horse, if unsound in his feet, however excellent his other points; since he could not turn a single one of them to good account."

- Xenophon, On Horsemanship, 355 BC

During the Middle Ages, farriery was considered part of the black-smith's trade and was passed down through apprenticeships. Blacksmiths were responsible for trimming and shoeing horses, as well as treating common hoof problems.

In the 19th century, farriery began to evolve into a more formalized profession. The first farrier schools were established, and the first farrier organizations were formed to set standards and promote the trade. Farriers began to specialize in different types of shoeing, such as therapeutic and performance shoeing.

In the 20th century, farriery continued to evolve with the introduction of new materials and technology. The use of aluminum and plastic shoes became popular, and the use of x-rays in hoof care became more widespread. Farriers also began collaborating more with veterinarians to provide a more comprehensive approach to hoof care.

Today, farriery is a respected profession that plays a vital role in the health and well-being of horses. Farriers are trained to understand the hoof's complex anatomy and can identify and treat a wide range of hoof problems. They work closely with horse owners and veterinarians to ensure that horses receive the best care for their hooves. Whether a horse is a companion animal or a high-performance athlete, the health and condition of its hooves are crucial to its overall health and performance.

A farrier plays a critical role in your horse's hoof care by providing a variety of services to maintain proper hoof function:

- **Trimming:** A farrier will perform regular hoof trimming to maintain proper hoof shape and balance. This involves removing any overgrown hoof wall and reshaping the foot to the correct form and balance. The farrier will also level the hoof and address any issues with the horse's conformation that may affect hoof health. Regular hoof trimming helps to keep the horse comfortable and prevents hoof problems from developing.

- **Shoeing:** If necessary, a farrier will also provide horseshoes to maintain proper hoof shape and function. This involves attaching shoes to the horse's hooves for added support, traction, protection, or correction. The farrier will select the appropriate type of shoe for the horse's needs, taking into account factors such as the horse's work and environment.

- **Hoof Care Advice:** A farrier will also provide horse owners with advice on hoof care. This may include information on nutrition, management practices, and environment to promote healthy hoof growth and prevent hoof problems from developing.

- **Identification and Treatment of Hoof Problems:** A farrier is trained to identify and address problems that may arise, such as diseases, infections, or injuries. They may work closely with a veterinarian and provide treatment options, such as specialty shoes, pads, or other therapeutic devices.

- **Safety Measures:** A farrier is trained to work with horses safely and professionally. They take the necessary safety measures to protect themselves and the horse from injury during trimming and shoeing.

What About Wild Horses?

In the wild, horses have evolved over 50 million years to be able to maintain their hooves. Adaptations have been observed in wild horses that help them to do this - a thick, tough hoof wall, a broad and deep sole, and a wide and durable frog. These adaptations allow them to traverse miles of challenging terrain without damaging their hooves.

Wild horses maintain their hooves through natural wear and tear. These rugged equines are constantly on the move, traveling with the herd to new areas in search of food and water. This constant movement helps them to wear down their hooves naturally, keeping them well-trimmed and shaped appropriately for their biological needs.

Wild horses also have a diet that is rich in nutrients that are essential for hoof health. They consume various grasses and plants, providing them with the vitamins and minerals they need to maintain strong and healthy hooves.

Genetic predispositions for poor hoof quality, or a likelihood to develop a chronic pathology, are often bred out of the herd. The unfortunate wild horse that develops severe laminitis, for example, simply becomes part of the food chain.

In stark contrast, domesticated horses are often kept in stalls and small pastures and may have lower activity levels, leading to overgrown hooves. A domestic diet can lead to nutritional deficiencies or obesity, which can negatively impact their hoof health. Careless breeding practices can perpetuate conformational challenges and poor-quality hooves within a bloodline. This is why domesticated horse owners must be attentive to their horse's hoof care needs and be proactive in preventative measures: to ensure that their horse's hooves are trimmed and shod as needed, their diet is balanced and nutritious, and debilitating diseases are kept at bay.

Importance of Hoof Care

Proper and timely hoof care is essential for horses' overall health and wellness. "No hoof, no horse," as the saying goes. When we contemplate the importance of paying close attention to your horse's hooves, here are a few things to consider:

- Hooves are the foundation of the horse's body: The hooves are the point of contact between the horse and the ground, supporting the horse's entire weight. Without healthy hooves, the horse's ability to move, work, and perform is compromised. Horses are athletic animals and require the ability to freely move to maintain proper bodily functions and health.

- Hooves are constantly growing and changing: Horses' hooves are continually growing, so they need regular maintenance to keep them in good shape. This includes regular trimming and shoeing to maintain proper hoof shape and function. The average hoof grows 1/4" to 3/8" per month, a whole new hoof each year.

- Hooves are susceptible to various disorders: Hooves are vulnerable to a wide range of ailments, such as laminitis, abscesses, etc. These disorders can cause severe pain and lameness, some even leading to long-term damage if not treated properly.

■ Hooves are an indicator of the horse's overall health: A horse suffering from a hoof disorder may also be experiencing other underlying health issues, like metabolic syndromes.

What Impacts Hoof Health?

Many factors can have a significant impact when it comes to the health of your horse's hooves. We must consider the whole horse and how different aspects of the animal contribute to a healthy foot. Here are some contributors to hoof health:

■ **Genetics:** A horse's genetics play a role in the overall health and condition of its hooves. Some horses are predisposed to hoof disorders due to their genetic makeup. Horses with poor conformation may be more likely to develop chronic hoof problems such as ringbone or the degeneration of tendons and ligaments. Conversely, some breeds of horses are known to have stronger hooves than others. The size and body weight of a horse relative to the size and strength of its hooves can also be a factor.

■ **Nutrition:** Nutrition is a crucial factor in maintaining hoof health. A diet deficient in essential nutrients such as biotin, zinc, and copper can lead to weak, brittle hooves. A diet too high in carbohydrates, especially non-structural carbohydrates (NSCs), can also lead to chronic hoof problems. It is essential to provide the horse with a balanced diet that meets its nutritional requirements.

■ **Environment:** The environment in which a horse is kept can also significantly impact hoof health. Horses kept on wet or muddy ground are more likely to develop bacterial infections, while those maintained on hard, rocky ground may be more likely to sustain hoof cracks and chips. Horses kept in stalls or small pens for extended periods may be more likely to develop problems due to lack of movement and exercise.

- **Management:** Proper management practices can help prevent hoof problems from developing. For example, providing horses with regular exercise and turnout can help promote healthy hoof growth. Additionally, regularly cleaning and disinfecting the horse's living area can help prevent bacterial and fungal infections from developing.

- **Disease:** Some diseases, such as Cushing's and other metabolic disorders, can also affect the hooves. These conditions can cause chronic hoof problems and may require specialized treatment.

Owner's Responsibility

Being a horse owner is an extraordinary and unique experience. It is a bond built on trust, mutual respect, and a deep understanding of the animal. As a horse owner, you are responsible for the health and comfort of a living being, which is both an honor and a privilege. This includes proper nutrition, exercise, grooming, and hoof care. Hooves are the foundation of the horse, and a lack of adequate maintenance can severely impact the horse's overall health.

Owning a horse is a lifelong commitment that requires a significant amount of time, effort, and financial investment. It is not a decision that should be taken lightly. But the rewards are immeasurable for those willing to make the commitment. The bond between horse and owner is exceptional and something to be cherished forever.

Being a responsible horse owner means being there for your horse through life's ups and downs, being their advocate, and providing them with the best care possible. Let's start with some specific steps you can take to be proactive in your horse's hoof care:

- **Work closely with a farrier:** Schedule regular hoof trimming and shoeing appointments with a farrier, and communicate openly with them about any concerns or issues you may have with your horse's hooves. Your farrier can provide valuable advice and guidance on maintaining healthy feet and preventing hoof problems from developing.

- **Stay informed:** Keep yourself informed about the latest hoof care practices and technologies. Read articles, books, and other resources about equine hoof care, and attend workshops or seminars to learn more about hoof health and management.

- **Pay attention to your horse's hooves:** Look at your horse's feet regularly and pay attention to any changes or signs of problems. Contact your farrier or veterinarian immediately if you notice any issues with your horse's hooves, such as lameness or injuries.

- **Provide proper nutrition:** Ensure your horse receives a balanced diet that meets its nutritional requirements, particularly for hoof health. Consult your veterinarian or nutritionist to determine the proper diet for your horse.

- **Proper Management:** Provide your horse with regular exercise and turnout, and keep their living area clean to limit the presence of bacteria and fungus. This can help promote healthy hoof growth and prevent hoof problems from developing.

- **Seek veterinary care if necessary:** If your horse shows signs of hoof problems, consult with a veterinarian as soon as possible. They can help determine the underlying cause of the problem and provide specialized treatment.

Stay Informed

We have developed an incredible bond with these magnificent creatures throughout history. As horse owners, we are responsible for caring for these animals and ensuring they live happy and healthy lives. One of the most fundamental aspects of horsemanship is hoof care, and horse owners must stay informed and knowledgeable about the latest practices and technologies in this field.

Hooves are one of the essential parts of a horse's anatomy, as they support the animal's weight and allow for movement. However, the feet are also one of the most vulnerable parts of a horse's body because they are exposed to the elements and are prone to injury and disease. This is why it is so vital for horse owners to continue learning and take an active role in their horse's hoof care.

One of the most effective ways to stay informed is speaking directly with your farrier about your horse's feet. Beyond that, reading books about equine hoof care can provide a wealth of knowledge. Not only will this give you a deeper understanding of the intricacies of horse care, but it will also help you make better decisions for your horse's health and happiness. Reading is also a great way to connect with other horse owners and experts in the field. Many books include resources and contact information for organizations and professionals who can provide additional support and guidance.

Books are a great place to start but are only one of many ways to stay informed. Horse owners can also attend seminars and workshops, consult with farriers and veterinarians, and participate in online communities dedicated to horse care. By staying up to date with the latest information, horse owners can ensure that their horses receive the best possible care.

In this book, you will find a general overview of the necessary aspects of maintaining your horse's hooves and information that will empower you to take charge of your horse's hoof health, including:

- **Anatomy and Physiology:** Detailed explanations of the different parts of the hoof and their functions, the horse's lower limb, tendons and ligaments, bones, and more, as well as how these parts come together in your horse. This knowledge will help you understand how your horse's feet work, grow, and change, the effects on your horse's movement and comfort, and the importance of regular hoof care.

- **Trimming and Shoeing:** A discussion of different types of hoof care, trimming, and shoeing. We present the pros and cons of barefoot vs. shod horses and how to determine which is suitable for you. You will learn about the different types of horseshoes, considerations for therapeutic shoeing, and how your horse's gait and conformation can be managed with specific shoe applications.

■ **Prevention and Maintenance:** Providing tips and guidelines for maintaining healthy hooves through proper nutrition and management. This information will help you to maintain a healthy environment, proper diet, and routines that promote healthy feet and prevent hoof problems from developing.

■ **Common Hoof Problems:** An introduction to common hoof conditions such as bacterial and fungal infections, diseases, and injuries. You will learn about the diagnosis, treatment options, and prevention of these conditions, as well as how to appropriately manage horses with these conditions. This information will empower you in your horse ownership by understanding how to identify and treat hoof problems.

■ **First Aid:** Take immediate action when your horse is experiencing lameness and potentially life-threatening hoof injuries. You will learn about the essential items to have on-hand for emergency hoof treatment and step-by-step instructions for rendering aid.

Overall, this book will provide horse owners with a comprehensive guide to equine hoof care and cover all aspects of hoof health. With in-depth knowledge shared by farriers and veterinarians from around the world, actionable tips, and how-to's, the information provided in this book should help horse owners understand the importance of proper hoof care, how to maintain healthy hooves and prevent hoof problems from developing.

Anatomy & Physiology

AS A HORSE OWNER, IT IS ESSENTIAL TO UNDERSTAND the anatomy and physiology of the equine hoof to properly care for and maintain your horse's hooves. The hoof is a complex structure that plays a vital role in the horse's overall health and wellness. It is responsible for supporting the horse's weight, providing traction, and protecting the sensitive internal structures of the foot.

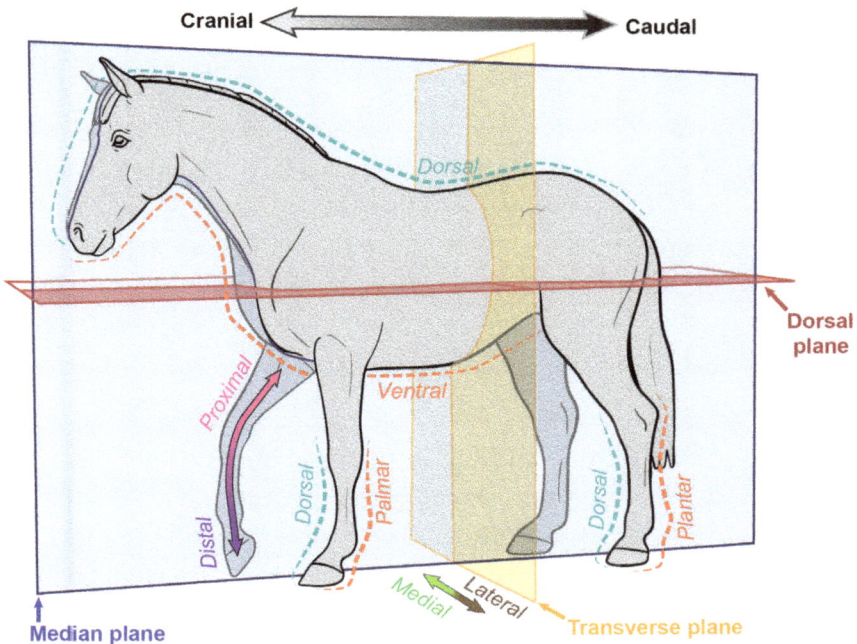

Understanding the basic anatomy of the hoof and lower limb is the first step in identifying and addressing any issues that may arise. The hoof, digital cushion, bones and joints, tendons and ligaments are all essential structures that support the horse's body and provide for ambulation. Each part of the hoof has a specific function and is critical to the overall health and function of the horse's anatomy.

In addition to the physical structure of the hoof, it is also essential to understand the physiology, or different functions, of the hoof. This includes the blood supply to the hoof and how it relates to hoof health, as well as the different layers of the hoof and how they contribute to hoof strength and flexibility. Understanding the physiology of the hoof also means being aware of the different types of hoof conformation, such as a club feet or under-run heels, and how they may affect hoof health and require special care.

With a deeper understanding of the structures of the hoof and limb, horse owners can take a proactive approach to hoof care and address any issues before they become serious problems. Expanding your knowledge and taking a proactive approach can provide the best possible care and ensure that your horse's hooves remain healthy and strong throughout life. Being familiar with anatomy and physiology is fundamental to the following:

- **Proper Hoof Trimming and Shoeing:** Understanding the anatomy of the hoof is essential for appropriate hoof trimming and shoeing. A farrier or a veterinarian familiar with the hoof's different structures can ensure that the horse's feet are trimmed and shod in a way that promotes proper hoof balance and function. A horse owner who understands the morphology, or structure, of the hoof can be sure their horse is properly maintained.

- **Identification of Hoof Disorders:** Understanding the anatomy and physiology of the hoof can also help identify hoof disorders and distortions. Understanding the different structures of the foot and how they work together makes it possible to identify abnormalities and diagnose hoof disorders more quickly and accurately.

- **Proper Treatment:** Knowing hoof anatomy and physiology can also aid in properly treating hoof disorders. For example, suppose a horse is diagnosed with laminitis. In that case, understanding the hoof's anatomy can help determine the best course of treatment, such as redistributing weight through therapeutic shoeing or addressing any underlying issues, such as poor nutrition, that may have contributed to the development of laminitis.

- **Prevention:** Understanding the anatomy and physiology of the hoof can also aid in the prevention of hoof disorders. By understanding the different structures of the hoof and how they work together, it is possible to identify potential problems before they occur and take steps to prevent them from developing.

- **Better Communication:** Understanding the hoof anatomy and physiology can facilitate communication between horse owners, farriers, and veterinarians. When all parties involved have a shared understanding of the hoof's structure and function, it allows for more accurate and efficient communication about the horse's health and the best course of action for care and treatment.

Hoof Structure

The equine hoof is a complex and intricate structure that plays a critical role in the overall health and well-being of the horse. The hoof is made up of many interconnected parts, each of which serves a specific purpose in supporting the horse's weight and providing traction. Let's take a look at the major components of the equine hoof:

Hoof Wall

The hoof wall is the hard, protective outer layer of the hoof. It encases the sensitive inner structures of the foot and provides support and protection. The hoof wall comprises several layers of keratin, the same protein that makes up human hair and nails. It is responsible for protecting the

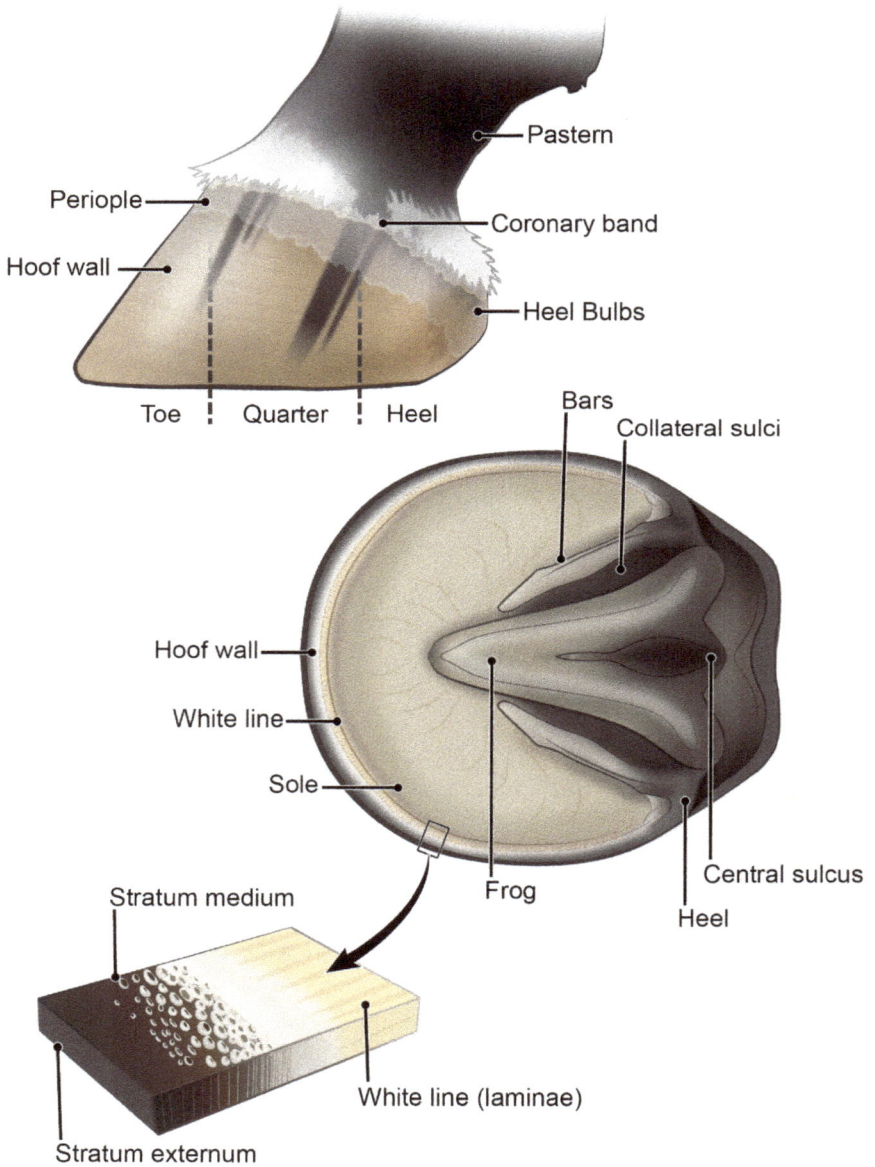

Pastern

Periople

Coronary band

Hoof wall

Heel Bulbs

Toe | Quarter | Heel

Bars

Collateral sulci

Hoof wall

White line

Sole

Central sulcus

Frog

Heel

Stratum medium

White line (laminae)

Stratum externum

inner structures of the hoof and providing support when the horse is moving. The hoof wall is divided into three distinct regions:

- **Toe:** The toe is the front portion of the hoof and is responsible for providing propulsion when the horse is moving. The toe is also responsible for maintaining the horse's balance and direction when moving. The toe "pillars" at either side of the toe are more rigid and densely packed with keratin, providing for weight bearing and structural support.

- **Quarters:** The quarters are the two sides of the hoof, located between the toe and the heel. They provide support and stability to the hoof and help to distribute the horse's weight evenly across the foot.

- **Heel:** The heel is the lower rear portion of the hoof and is responsible for absorbing shock when the horse's foot strikes the ground. It also helps to prevent the horse from slipping by providing traction.

The hoof wall is the outermost protective casing of the equine hoof and is made up of several different layers. The wall itself is composed of the periople, the stratum externum, and the stratum medium.

The periople is a thin, waxy layer that covers the hoof wall and helps to protect it from moisture and debris. It also helps to retain the hoof's natural oils to keep the hoof supple and pliable.

The stratum externum is the outermost layer of hoof wall and comprises tightly packed parallel keratin fibers. This layer is responsible for providing the hoof with its strength and durability.

The stratum medium is the middle layer of the hoof wall and is made up of more loosely packed keratin fibers. This layer helps to cushion the hoof and provides a degree of flexibility.

The stratum internum, also known as the laminae, is the innermost layer that is responsible for attaching the hoof wall to the coffin bone and providing the primary support for the horse's weight. It is composed of delicate, interlocking layers of tissue called laminar corium and dermal papillae. The stratum internum is richly supplied with blood vessels, nerves, and sensitive cells, which makes it very susceptible to injury and disease. It is also the most crucial layer for maintaining the integrity and strength of the hoof wall and is essential for the overall health and well-being of the horse.

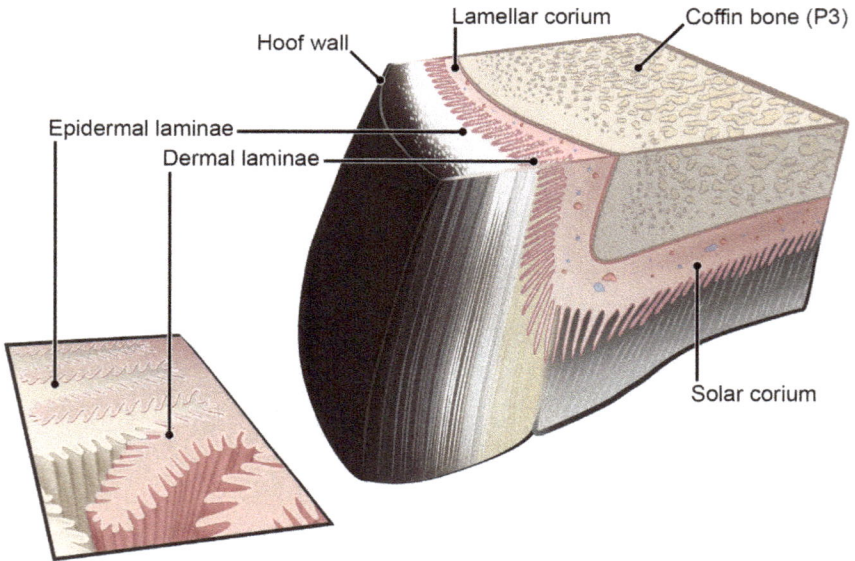

The laminae are made up of millions of tiny, interlocking cells called laminar cells. These cells are arranged in a delicate, interlocking pattern, much like a jigsaw puzzle, allowing flexibility and movement.

The laminar cells are attached to the coffin bone via a series of small blood vessels called the digital vasculature. This vasculature provides the laminar cells with the necessary nutrients and oxygen to function correctly. The digital vasculature also helps to remove waste products and toxins from the hoof.

When the laminar cells are healthy, they provide a strong and stable connection between the pedal bone and the hoof wall. This allows the horse to move comfortably and efficiently. However, when the laminar cells become damaged or diseased, the connection between the pedal bone and the hoof wall can weaken, leading to severe lameness and other hoof problems.

Several factors can contribute to damage or disease of the laminar cells. These include poor nutrition, injury, infection, and chronic hoof conditions such as laminitis. It is vital for horse owners to be aware of these risk factors and to take steps to prevent and treat hoof problems to maintain the health of the laminar cells. Providing regular hoof trims for your horse can protect its feet from excessive stress and trauma to the laminae. Maintaining a clean environment can prevent infections.

The laminae play a vital role in the function and health of the equine hoof. Understanding the importance of these cells, and taking steps to protect them, is crucial for horse owners who want to keep their horses healthy, comfortable, and sound.

Coronary Band & Corium

There are other structures within the hoof that are imperative to the growth and function of the hoof wall. These include the coronary band, the laminar corium, and the solar corium.

The coronary band is the area of the hoof where the hoof wall meets the skin and hair of the horse's leg. It is responsible for producing new hoof wall and is essential for the growth and repair of the hoof. The coronary band also plays a role in the blood supply to the foot, which is critical for hoof health.

The corium is a layer of tissue located inside the hoof wall and sole of an equine hoof. It is responsible for producing the cells that make up the laminae and sole and supplying the hoof with the necessary blood and nutrients. The corium comprises several layers of cells, including the basal cells, which divide and differentiate to form the various structures of the hoof, and the dermal papillae, which are responsible for the formation of the laminar connection between the hoof wall and the underlying bone. The corium is also rich in blood vessels and nerves, which are necessary for the proper growth and function of the hoof wall. The corium plays a crucial role in maintaining the integrity of the hoof wall. Any damage or disruption to the corium can lead to serious hoof problems, such as laminitis or hoof abscesses.

The laminar corium is the region of corium tissue that attaches the hoof wall to the front of the coffin bone. The solar corium is the layer of tissue that attaches the sole to the bottom of the coffin bone.

Sole

The sole is the bottom of the hoof that comes into contact with the ground and is responsible for protecting the sensitive inner structures of the hoof. It comprises a thick layer of keratin that provides a barrier against the external environment and helps protect the foot's internal systems. The sole is also responsible for providing traction and weight-bearing support when the horse moves.

The outermost layer of the sole is the stratum externum, a thick, keratinized layer that provides a barrier against external trauma and moisture. This layer is made up of tightly packed, interlocking cells that are resistant to wear and tear.

Beneath the stratum externum is the stratum medium, a softer, more flexible layer that helps absorb shock and distribute weight evenly across the sole. This layer is made up of loosely packed cells that are rich in blood vessels and nerves.

The innermost layer of the sole is the stratum internum, also known as the sensitive sole. This layer is made up of highly sensitive and delicate tissue responsible for sensing pressure and providing proprioception, or the ability to sense the position and movement of the hoof. The stratum internum is rich in blood vessels, nerves, and specialized cells called Pacinian corpuscles, which are responsible for detecting pressure changes.

Frog

The frog is another essential structure of the equine hoof. The frog is a triangular-shaped structure located at the back of the hoof composed of soft tissue that helps to distribute weight and support the heel of the hoof. It is critical in providing shock absorption and support when the horse's foot strikes the ground.

The frog also helps pump blood back up the leg when the horse moves, which helps maintain healthy blood circulation. The frog is a vital structure in the hoof and plays a crucial role in maintaining proper hoof function, circulation, balance, and support.

A healthy frog should be pliable, resilient, and free from any signs of infection or disease. A diseased frog can become infected, shriveled and atrophied, causing pain for the horse and greatly reducing its abilities to absorb shock or circulate blood.

Heel Bulbs & Digital Cushion

The heel bulbs are located above the heel and are responsible for providing support and cushioning when the horse's foot strikes the ground. The heel bulbs are the external protrusions of the digital cushion, a thick pad of fibrous tissue located in the back of the hoof.

The digital cushion is a specialized structure within the equine hoof, located between the frog and the heel bulbs in the rear portion of the foot. It is made up of a complex network of connective tissue and blood vessels responsible for reducing the impact of the horse's weight on the hoof as it strikes the ground, as well as aiding in blood circulation.. The the connective tissue helps to distribute the load and absorb shock, while blood vessels within the cushion provide oxygen and nutrients to the surrounding tissue When your horse's heel strikes the ground, the digital cushion is compressed, dispersing blood throughout the hoof and back up the limb to the heart. When the foot leaves the ground, the compression of the digital cushion is released, allowing newly oxygenated blood to flow into the hoof. This function is one reason proper exercise is critical to hoof health, as movement allows for more blood circulation to the hoof. The digital cushion is essential for maintaining the integrity and health of the hoof, and its proper function is vital for the overall soundness and well-being of the horse. Issues with the digital cushion, such as inflammation or degeneration, can lead to lameness and other hoof problems. So, regular hoof care and veterinary check-ups are necessary to ensure the digital cushion is properly functioning.

The equine hoof comprises several parts, each with its unique function and role in supporting the horse's weight and providing traction. The hoof wall, laminae, sole, digital cushion, and corium all work together to ensure effective ground contact, movement, and the protection of internal structures. In addition to these structural components, the hoof wall also contains a number of blood vessels, nerves, and lymphatic vessels that are important for maintaining the health and well-being of the hoof. Understanding the functions of each of these parts and how they work together will help horse owners to be able to properly care for their horse's hooves and prevent hoof problems from developing.

Bones

The equine limb is a complex system of bones, muscles, tendons, and ligaments that support the horse's weight and allow for movement. Hoof care is generally concerned with the distal limb of a horse, which refers to the lower portion of the horse's leg below the knee or hock, including the hoof and the bones that comprise the foot. Adequate and timely trimming and shoeing of a horse's hooves can ensure that these bones are maintained in proper alignment, allowing them to move and function correctly. The distal limb of a horse is made up of several bones, which include:

The Cannon Bone

The cannon bone, also known as the metacarpus (fore limb) or metatarsus (hind limb), is the long bone between the knee or hock and the fetlock joint in the horse's front and hind legs, respectively. It is the most prominent bone in the horse's lower limb and is responsible for supporting the horse's weight and providing leverage for movement. To be more specific, the cannon bone is the 3rd metacarpal bone, the anatomical equivalent of your middle finger. The splint bones (2nd and 4th metacarpals), run along either side of the cannon bone and are the vestigial remnants of prehistoric horses' additional toes.

The cannon bone is divided into several parts, including the proximal extremity (top), the diaphysis (shaft), and the distal extremity (bottom).

The proximal extremity is where the cannon bone attaches to the knee (or hock) joint and contains a slight depression called the trochlea. The

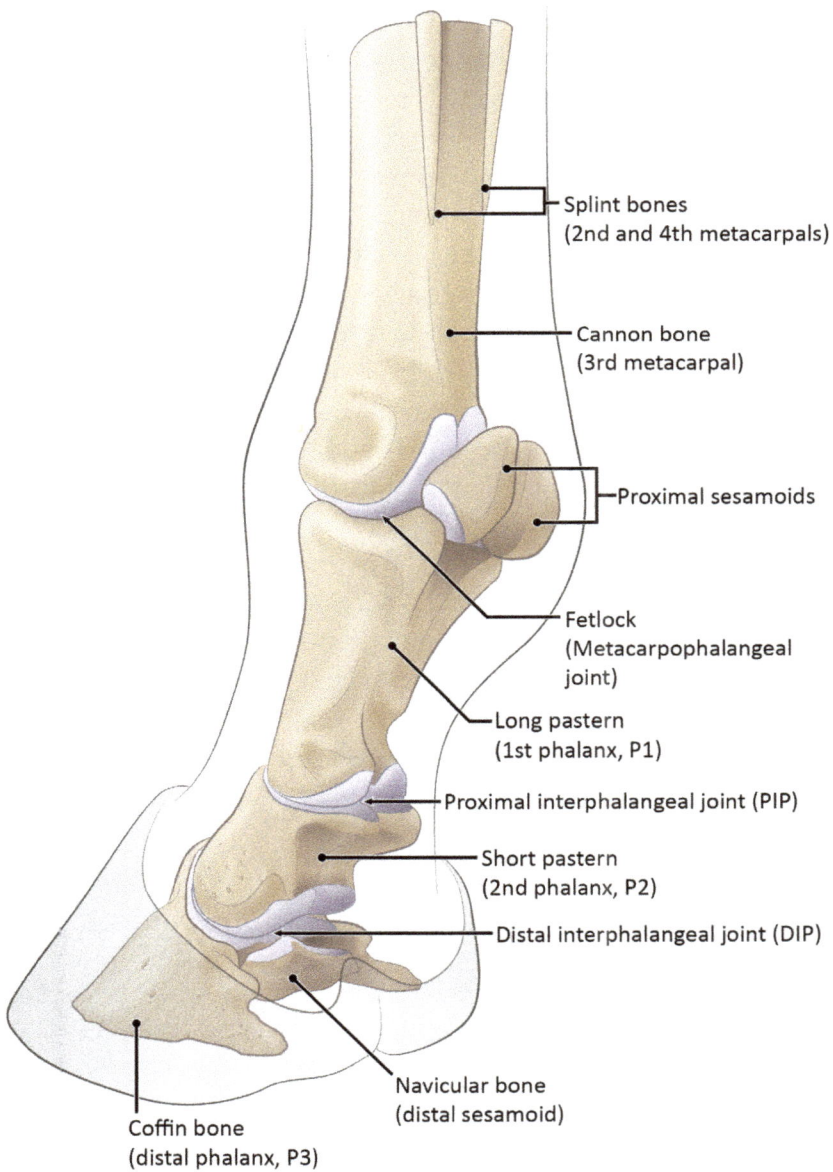

Splint bones
(2nd and 4th metacarpals)

Cannon bone
(3rd metacarpal)

Proximal sesamoids

Fetlock
(Metacarpophalangeal
joint)

Long pastern
(1st phalanx, P1)

Proximal interphalangeal joint (PIP)

Short pastern
(2nd phalanx, P2)

Distal interphalangeal joint (DIP)

Navicular bone
(distal sesamoid)

Coffin bone
(distal phalanx, P3)

diaphysis is the longest and thickest part of the bone and is responsible for bearing the horse's weight. It is also where the digital flexor tendons run, which are responsible for the horse's ability to lift its leg. The distal extremity is where the cannon bone attaches to the fetlock joint and contains two small protuberances called the medial and lateral tuberosity.

The Long and Short Pastern Bones

The pastern bones are located between the fetlock joint and the coffin bone in the equine hoof. The long pastern bone, also known as the first phalanx or P1, is the uppermost bone in the pastern region. It connects to the cannon bone at the fetlock joint. The short pastern bone, also known as the second phalanx or P2, is the lowermost bone in the pastern region. It connects to the coffin bone (third phalanx or P3) at the coffin joint. Together, the long and short pastern bones form the pastern joint, which acts as a shock absorber for the horse's weight and movement.

The angle and conformation of the pastern bones play a significant role in the horse's overall soundness and movement. A longer, sloping pastern can provide more shock absorption, while a shorter, upright pastern can make the horse more prone to injury. The pastern bones also help to support the horse's weight and are important in maintaining the proper balance of the hoof. The pastern bones are also important as they are involved in the horse's gait and can provide important information about its overall health and soundness.

The Coffin Bone

The coffin bone, also known as the distal phalanx or P3, is the third and lowest bone in the horse's hoof. It is located inside the foot, and is the primary weight-bearing bone within the hoof. The coffin bone is roughly triangular, with a concave surface on the bottom, which fits into the concave sole of the hoof, and a convex surface on the top which supports the sensitive laminar tissue and the hoof wall.

The coffin bone is attached to the short pastern bone above it and is supported by the navicular bone, deep digital flexor tendon, and the suspensory ligament. It is also surrounded by the hoof wall, the sole, and the frog, which help to protect it and provide shock absorption.

Abnormalities in the coffin bone, such as fractures or laminitis, can cause severe lameness and pain in the horse and require prompt attention and treatment.

The Navicular Bone

The navicular bone, also known as the distal sesamoid bone, is located in the distal limb of a horse within the hoof. It is a small bone suspended under the coffin bone and the short pastern bone. The navicular bone is responsible for helping to support the weight of the horse and transmit forces through the hoof. It also plays a role in the flexion and extension of the foot during movement.

The navicular bone is a small but essential structure supported by several tendons and ligaments. These include the deep digital flexor tendon, which runs from the muscles in the horse's leg and attaches to the coffin bone, gliding over the navicular bone like a sling. The impar ligament attaches the navicular bone to the coffin bone, and a suspensory ligament attaches the navicular bone to the short pastern bone.

In some cases, the navicular bone can become damaged, leading to a condition known as navicular syndrome, where the horse experiences pain in the heel area and can develop lesions on the deep digital flexor tendon.

The Proximal Sesamoids

The proximal sesamoids are two small bones on the upper rear of the fetlock joint. The proximal sesamoids play a crucial role in the horse's movement by acting as pulleys for the tendons that pass over them. They also help to distribute the weight of the horse's body through the hoof. In addition, they act as shock absorbers by absorbing the impact of the horse's weight as it strikes the ground.

The proximal sesamoids are also crucial for providing support and stability, keeping the tendons and ligaments in their proper position, which is essential for the overall health of the hoof and distal limb.

Joints

The distal limb of a horse, also known as the lower limb or lower extremity, is the portion of the horse's leg below the carpus ("knee") or tarsus (hock) and made up of several joints that work together to support the horse's weight and allow for movement. The distal limb below the carpus and tarsus are nearly identical on both fore and hind legs.

A joint is where two or more bones come together in the body. The bones are held together by soft tissue, such as ligaments and cartilage, which help to hold the bones in place and allow for movement. The joints in the body are categorized based on their structure and function, with three main types: fibrous, cartilaginous, and synovial.

Fibrous joints, also known as synarthroses, are immovable joints held together by fibrous connective tissue. These joints are found in the head, between the bones of the skull, and provide strength and stability to the skull while protecting the brain.

Cartilaginous joints, also known as amphiarthroses, are slightly movable joints held together by cartilage. These joints are found in the spine, where discs of cartilage connect the vertebrae. They provide stability to the spine while also allowing for some movement.

Synovial joints, also known as diarthroses, are freely movable joints, the most common type of joint in the body. They are found in the limbs, where bones are connected by ligaments and surrounded by a synovial membrane. The synovial membrane produces synovial fluid, which lubricates the joint and helps to reduce friction. The bones are also cushioned by cartilage, which helps to absorb shock and distribute weight. Joint injections and oral supplements containing hyaluronic acid aim to provide your horse's joints with more synovial fluid. Injections of platelet rich plasma (PRP) can be effective in treating arthritis and healing the soft tissues in the joint.

There are several types of synovial joints, including:

- **Plane joint (arthroidal):** These joints are flat and allow for sliding or gliding movements, such as between the carpal/tarsal bones.

- **Hinge joint (ginglymus):** These joints allow for movement in one plane only, like the hinge on a door. Examples include the fetlock and interphalangeal joints.

- **Pivot joint (trochoid):** These joints allow for rotation around a central axis, such as between the atlas and axis vertebrae in the neck.

- **Ball-and-socket joint (spheroid):** These joints are the most mobile and allow for movement in multiple planes. Examples include the hip and shoulder joints.

There are six types of joint movement:

- **Flexion:** This is the movement that decreases the angle between two bones. For example, when you bring your hand closer to your shoulder, you are flexing your elbow joint.

- **Extension:** This is the opposite of flexion, where the angle between two bones increases. When you straighten your leg, you are extending your knee joint.

- **Abduction:** This is the movement that takes a body part away from the midline of the body. If you raise your arm out to the side, you are abducting your shoulder joint.

- **Adduction:** This is the opposite of abduction, where a body part is moved towards the midline of the body. For example, when you bring your legs together, you are adducting your hip joint.

- **Rotation:** This is the movement where a bone rotates around its axis. When you turn your head to look over your shoulder, you are rotating your neck.

- **Circumduction:** This is the movement where the end of a body part moves in a circular path, such as when you swing your arm in a circle. It is a combination of flexion, extension, abduction, and adduction.

The main synovial joints of the distal limb are the fetlock, pastern, and coffin joints. The tendons and ligaments in the distal limb help to stabilize these joints and protect them from injury, as well as supporting the horse's weight and allowing for movement. It's essential to keep these joints and the surrounding tissue healthy by providing proper care and nutrition and avoiding overuse and trauma.

Carpus

The carpus, also known as the "knee," is in the center of the horse's front legs, between the cannon bone and the forearm. It is a composite joint made up of the articulation of two rows of small bones that lie between the radius and ulna (forearm) and the metacarpal bones (cannon and splint bones). The carpus consists of three primary articulations: the antebrachiocarpal joint, the middle carpal joint, and the carpometacarpal joint.

The carpus is designed to allow for a wide range of motion, including flexion and extension, as well as some rotation. This is important for the horse as it allows them to move in various ways, such as galloping, trotting, and jumping. The joints are also designed to withstand the heavy weight and impact of the horse's movements.

Proper conformation and function of the carpal joints are important for the overall health and performance of the horse. Abnormalities in the conformation or operation of the carpus can lead to lameness and other problems. Regular veterinary examinations, farrier check-ups, and proper training and conditioning can help maintain the carpus' health and prevent issues from arising.

Tarsus

The tarsus, also known as the hock, is a complex joint located at the back of the horse's hind legs, between the metatarsal, the tibia, and the fibula. The tarsus is a composite joint made up of several bones, including the talus, calcaneus, and cuboid bones. These bones are held together by various ligaments, tendons, and muscles, which work together to provide support and stability to the joint.

The tarsus is responsible for the flexion and extension of the hind limb, allowing the horse to move forward and providing shock absorption when the horse is running or jumping. The joint is also responsible for the horse's ability to pivot and turn, as well as make complex sideways movements.

The tarsal joints are susceptible to a variety of problems, such as arthritis, tendon and ligament injuries, and bone spavin (a degenerative

Palmar view

Dorsal view

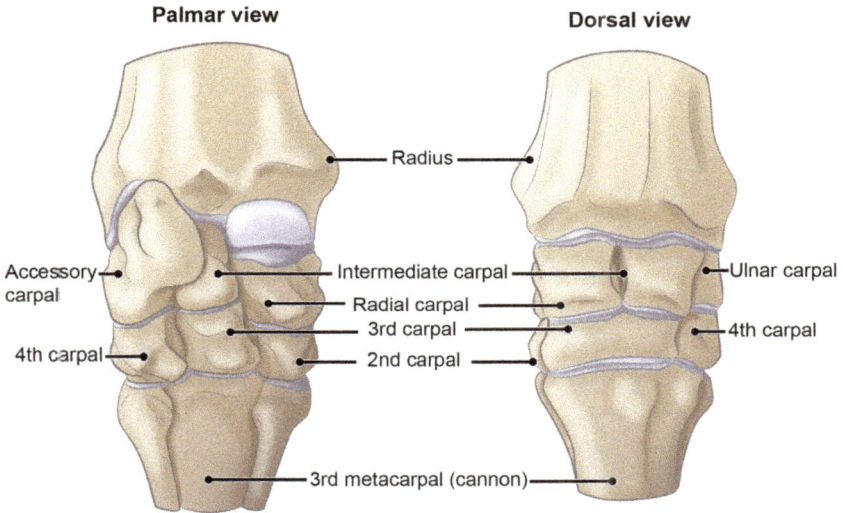

Radius

Accessory carpal

Intermediate carpal

Ulnar carpal

Radial carpal

4th carpal

3rd carpal

2nd carpal

4th carpal

3rd metacarpal (cannon)

Radius

Accessory carpal

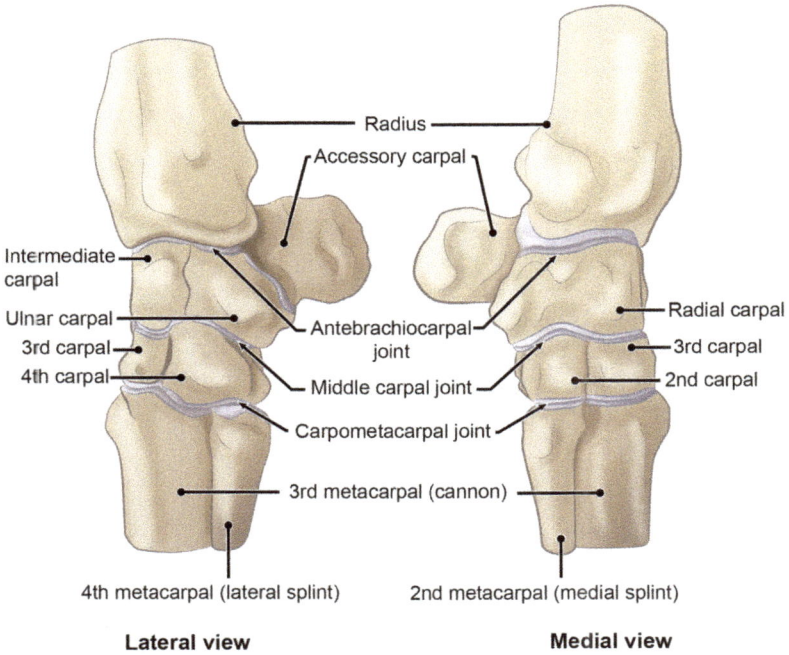

Intermediate carpal

Ulnar carpal

3rd carpal

4th carpal

Antebrachiocarpal joint

Radial carpal

3rd carpal

2nd carpal

Middle carpal joint

Carpometacarpal joint

3rd metacarpal (cannon)

4th metacarpal (lateral splint)

2nd metacarpal (medial splint)

Lateral view

Medial view

Plantar view   **Dorsal view**

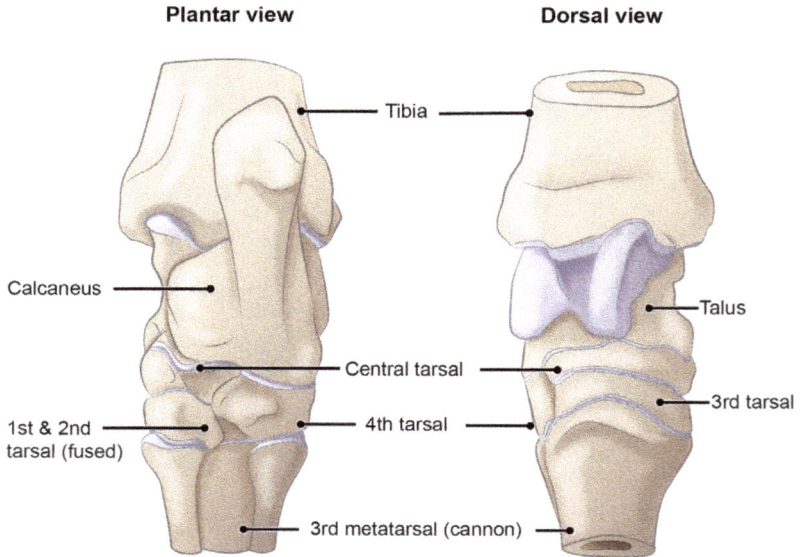

Tibia

Calcaneus

Central tarsal

Talus

3rd tarsal

1st & 2nd tarsal (fused)

4th tarsal

3rd metatarsal (cannon)

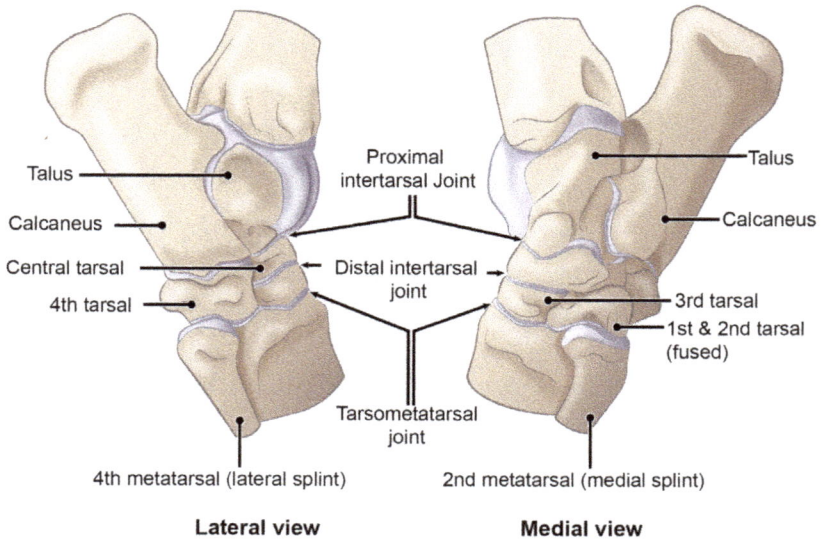

Talus

Proximal intertarsal Joint

Talus

Calcaneus

Calcaneus

Central tarsal

Distal intertarsal joint

3rd tarsal

4th tarsal

1st & 2nd tarsal (fused)

Tarsometatarsal joint

4th metatarsal (lateral splint)

2nd metatarsal (medial splint)

Lateral view   **Medial view**

condition of the joint). These conditions can lead to lameness and pain and can be diagnosed through a combination of physical examination, radiography, and other diagnostic tools.

The Fetlock

The fetlock joint, also known as the "ankle" or the metacarpophalangeal joint, is located between the long bone of the lower leg (the cannon bone, or metacarpal/tarsal) and the first bone of the digit (the long pastern, or P1). The fetlock is a hinge joint, allowing flexion and extension but only allowing minimal rotation, adduction, or abduction.

The joint is surrounded by several important structures that help to support and stabilize it. The joint capsule is a tough, fibrous membrane that surrounds the joint and helps to hold it in place. Inside the joint capsule, several ligaments help to keep the bones together and prevent excessive movement. These include the collateral ligaments, which run along the sides of the joint, and the suspensory ligament, which runs down the back of the cannon bone and splits behind and underneath the joint to help support the weight of the horse.

The joint also contains a small amount of synovial fluid, which acts as a lubricant to smooth bones' movement. Additionally, several bursae, or fluid-filled sacs, are located around the joint that help cushion and protect it from impact.

The fetlock joint is also surrounded by several tendons that help to control and stabilize its movement. These include the flexor tendons, which run down the back of the leg and help to flex the joint, and the extensor tendons, which run down the front of the leg and help to extend the joint.

Overall, the fetlock joint plays a critical role in the movement and function of the horse, allowing for the complex and coordinated movements necessary for walking, running, and jumping. It is a complex structure subject to a wide range of stresses and strains, and horse owners need to be aware of its importance and take steps to maintain its health and function through proper care and management.

Cannon bone (3rd metacarpal)

Deep digital flexor tendon

Joint capsule

Synovial bursa

Collateral ligament

Synovial bursa

Proximal sesamoids

Articular cartilage

Palmar annular ligament

Proximal digital annular ligament

Superficial digital flexor tendon

Long pastern (1st phalanx)

The Pastern Joint

The pastern joint, or the proximal interphalangeal (PIP) joint, is located between the first and second phalanges (P1 and P2) of the horse's digit. It is a hinge joint, which allows for flexion and extension of the digit. The articulation between the distal end of the first phalanx and the proximal end of the second phalanx forms the joint.

The PIP joint is surrounded by a fibrous capsule lined with a synovial membrane. This membrane produces synovial fluid, which lubricates the joint to reduce friction. The joint is also supported by several ligaments, including the collateral ligaments, which run along the sides of the joint and provide stability.

The PIP joint is responsible for a significant portion of the horse's weight bearing, particularly during the stance phase of the stride. It also plays a role in shock absorption during movement. Abnormalities or injuries to the PIP joint can lead to lameness, pain, and decreased performance. Common issues include arthritis, ligament or tendon injuries, and osteochondrosis. Proper hoof care, farrier care, and management can help prevent PIP joint issues.

The Coffin Joint

The coffin joint, or distal interphalangeal (DIP) joint, is the joint located at the bottom of the horse's short pastern bone (P2) and the top of the coffin bone (distal phalanx or P3). This joint is responsible for the flexion and extension of the horse's foot, which allows for movement and weight bearing. The DIP joint is a hinge joint that allows for movement in one plane, flexion and extension.

The DIP joint is surrounded by several important structures that help to support and protect it. The collateral ligaments are located on either side of the joint and help to prevent excessive side-to-side movement. The deep digital flexor tendon runs along the back of the pastern, attaches to the bottom of the coffin bone, and helps flex the joint and provide support. The impar ligament runs across the back of the DIP joint and helps to prevent hyperextension. The DIP joint is also supplied by blood vessels and nerves that help to nourish and innervate the joint.

Problems with the DIP joint can lead to lameness and poor performance. Common issues include arthritis, inflammation, and degeneration of the joint.

Each of these joints plays a crucial role in the overall function of the distal limb and the horse's ability to move and support its weight. When considering the necessity of regular hoof care, ensuring that your horse's hooves are properly trimmed and balanced promotes good joint health and significantly reduces the danger of crippling arthritis.

Tendons & Ligaments

Tendons and ligaments are both types of connective tissue that play a vital role in supporting the horse's musculoskeletal system. Tendons connect muscle to bone, while ligaments connect bone to bone. Together, they work to stabilize joints and allow for movement.

The tendons in the distal limb of a horse are responsible for transmitting the force generated by the muscles to the bones, allowing the horse to move. The deep digital flexor tendon and the superficial digital flexor tendon are the two main tendons that run down the back of the leg and connect to the bones of the hoof. These tendons, along with the extensor tendon on the front of the leg, allow the horse to flex and extend the joints of the distal limb, allowing it to walk, trot, canter, and gallop.

Ligaments, on the other hand, provide stability to the joints by connecting bone to bone. They help to keep the bones in proper alignment and prevent excessive movement. In the distal limb, the most important ligaments are the ones that connect the bones of the pastern, fetlock, and coffin joints. These ligaments and tendons allow the horse to bear weight, balance, and move.

It is important to note that tendons and ligaments are not as well-vascularized as muscles, which means they have a lower blood supply and heal slower. Injuries to tendons and ligaments can take months or even years to heal, and sometimes they may never fully recover. This is why it is crucial to monitor the horse's movement, be aware of any signs of lameness, and provide proper care, nutrition, and exercise to minimize the risk of injuries.

Tendons and ligaments play a significant role in the function of the horse's distal limb. They are responsible for transmitting force and providing stability to the joints, allowing the horse to move and bear weight. The major tendons and ligaments in the horse's distal limb include:

The Deep Digital Flexor Tendon

The deep digital flexor tendon, or DDFT, is a large and powerful tendinous structure located within the limbs of horses. It originates from the upper leg muscles and runs through the lower limb, gliding over the navicular

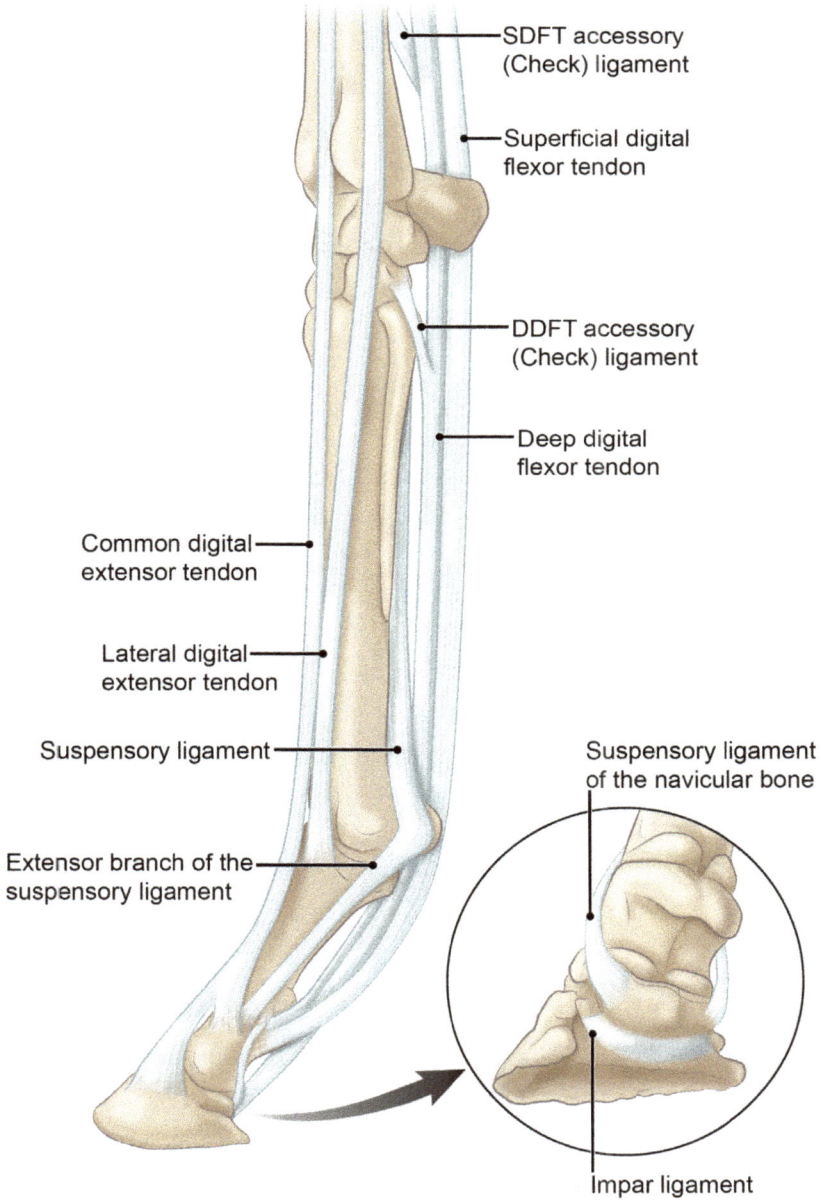

SDFT accessory (Check) ligament

Superficial digital flexor tendon

DDFT accessory (Check) ligament

Deep digital flexor tendon

Common digital extensor tendon

Lateral digital extensor tendon

Suspensory ligament

Extensor branch of the suspensory ligament

Suspensory ligament of the navicular bone

Impar ligament

bone and attaching to the coffin bone (P3). The tendon is responsible for flexing the joints of the lower limb, particularly the coffin (DIP) and pastern (PIP) joints, allowing the horse to lift its hooves and move them forward during locomotion.

The deep digital flexor tendon is composed of fibrous connective tissue. It is surrounded by a thin sheath of synovial fluid that helps to lubricate and protect the tendon as it glides through the various structures of the lower limb. It is a crucial structure for the normal function of the horse's limb, as it provides the necessary tension and support for the horse to perform various movements such as walking, trotting, cantering, and jumping.

However, the constant stress and strain placed on the DDFT make it prone to injuries such as strains, tears, or ruptures. These injuries can range from mild to severe, leading to lameness and decreased performance. Poor conformation, overuse, and poor hoof balance can all contribute to DDFT injuries by placing extreme amounts of unnatural stress on the tendon. An overgrown hoof increases leverage and can easily add hundreds of pounds of pressure to the DDFT, greatly increasing the likelihood of injuries.

Proper hoof care, regular exercise, and regular veterinary check-ups can help to prevent DDFT injuries. If a horse is suspected of having an injury to the DDFT, a veterinarian will typically perform a physical examination and may also use diagnostic imaging such as radiography or ultrasonography to confirm the diagnosis and assess the extent of the injury. Treatment options may include rest, physiotherapy, and supportive shoeing. In severe cases, surgery may be necessary.

The Superficial Digital Flexor Tendon

The superficial digital flexor tendon, or SDFT, is one of the main tendons that run down the back of the horse's leg, along with the deep digital flexor tendon. The SDFT originates at the muscles of the upper limb and runs down the back of the leg, inserting at the back of the long and short pastern bones. Its primary function is to flex the fetlock joint, which allows the horse to lift its foot and perform various gaits. The SDFT also helps to stabilize the fetlock joint and plays a role in maintaining the horse's balance and posture.

The superficial digital flexor tendon is the more prominent and out-ermost of the two flexor tendons, hence the name. It is also more prone to injury, as it is more exposed and has to work harder during certain movements such as jumping and running. Injuries to the SDFT can range from mild strains to complete tears, resulting in lameness and reduced performance. Treatment options vary depending on the severity of the injury but may include rest, physiotherapy, and in some cases, surgery.

The Extensor Tendons

The extensor tendons in a horse are responsible for extending the joints in the limb, particularly the fetlock joint. The main extensor tendon in the horse is called the common digital extensor tendon (CDET). It orig-inates at elbow level, runs down the front of the leg, and inserts at the extensor process of the coffin bone. The CDET is responsible for extend-ing the joints during movement, such as when the horse is running or jumping.

The CDET is composed of multiple smaller tendons, including the lateral digital extensor (LDE) and the extensor indicis (EI) tendons. The LDE is the most superficial of the tendons and is responsible for extend-ing the fetlock joint, while the EI is responsible for extending the pastern joint.

The CDET is surrounded by a fibrous sheath called the tendon sheath, which helps to lubricate and protect the tendon during movement. The tendon sheath is lined with synovial fluid, which helps to reduce friction and wear on the tendon during activity.

The extensor tendons coordinate with the flexor tendons, such as the deep digital flexor tendon (DDFT) and the superficial digital flexor tendon (SDFT), to control movement and support the horse's weight. Damage or injury to the extensor tendons can result in lameness and, if left untreated, can lead to chronic pain and disability. Proper care, including regular exer-cise, quality shoeing, and regular veterinary check-ups, can help to prevent injury and maintain the health of the extensor tendons.

The Suspensory Ligament

The suspensory ligament of a horse is a complex structure that helps to support and stabilize the horse's distal limb, particularly the fetlock joint. It is a strong, fibrous band that runs from the back of the cannon bone, just below the knee (carpus) or hock (tarsus), down the back of the fetlock joint, and bifurcates and attaches to the front of the pastern bone.

The primary function of the suspensory ligaments is to help support the horse's weight and act as shock absorbers when the horse is moving. They help distribute the horse's weight evenly across the limb and prevent excessive stress on any one area of the limb. They also help maintain the horse's balance and stability and prevent it from overreaching or interfering with its legs. Additionally, they help control the joints' movement and prevent excessive flexion or extension.

The suspensory ligament also plays a role in the horse's movement, particularly in activities such as jumping and galloping. The ligament can store and release energy, which helps to propel the horse forward and upward during movement.

The suspensory ligament is made up of both elastic and inelastic fibers. The elastic fibers allow for a certain amount of stretch and flexibility, which is important for the horse to move and bear weight on the limb. The inelastic fibers provide stability and support for the limb, helping to prevent excessive movement of the fetlock joint. Injuries to the suspensory ligament, such as strains or tears, can be serious and require prompt and proper treatment to ensure a full recovery.

Collateral Ligaments

The collateral ligaments in the limb of a horse are located on either side of the joints and are responsible for providing stability to the joints. These ligaments connect the bones within the joint and prevent excessive movement in any one direction. The collateral ligaments are particularly important for the fetlock joint, which bears a significant weight and is subject to a lot of stress during movement.

The medial collateral ligament is located on the inside of the joint and helps to prevent valgus (outward) deviation of the joint. The lateral collateral ligament, on the other hand, is located on the outside of the joint and helps to prevent varus (inward) deviation of the joint. Together, these ligaments maintain proper alignment of the bones within the joint and help distribute weight and stress evenly.

Damage to these ligaments can occur due to injury, overuse, or chronic conditions such as arthritis. In such cases, the horse may experience lameness and pain in the affected joint. Treatment options may include rest, medication, physical therapy, and in severe cases, surgery. To prevent damage to the collateral ligaments, it is vital to maintain proper hoof balance, provide adequate exercise and nutrition, and address any underlying conditions such as conformation issues or chronic inflammation.

Annular Ligaments

Annular ligaments are a group of fibrous tissue that encircle and support joints within the distal limb of a horse. They are located around the fetlock, pastern, and coffin joints and play an essential role in maintaining the stability and integrity of these joints.

The annular ligament of the fetlock joint is located around the joint capsule and is responsible for providing support and limiting the range of motion at the fetlock. The annular ligament of the pastern joint is located around the proximal interphalangeal joint, which helps support the pastern and limits the range of motion at this joint. The annular ligament of the coffin joint is located around the distal interphalangeal joint, which helps support the coffin bone and limits the range of motion at this joint.

The annular ligaments are also crucial for maintaining the blood supply to the joints and surrounding tissues. They contain small blood vessels that help to nourish the joint and surrounding tissues.

Damage or injury to the annular ligaments can occur due to overuse, trauma, or disease, leading to joint instability and lameness. Treatment for annular ligament injury may include rest, physiotherapy, and in severe cases, surgery. To prevent injuries, it is vital to maintain proper hoof care and provide regular exercise and conditioning for the horse.

Vasculature

The blood supply to any given area of the body is of vital importance to the overall health and function of that area. In the case of the equine hoof, the blood supply plays a crucial role in maintaining the health and integrity of the hoof structure. The hoof is made up of many different components, each with its own unique function and properties. Each of these structures is supported and nourished by the blood supply to the hoof.

The blood supply to the hoof begins with the coronary band, the area at the top of the foot where the hairline meets the hoof. This band is rich in blood vessels and is responsible for nourishing the growing hoof tissue. The blood vessels then travel behind the hoof wall, nourishing the sensitive laminar tissue that lies within. This tissue is responsible for connecting the hoof wall to the coffin bone, and without a proper blood supply, it can become damaged and lead to conditions such as laminitis.

The blood supply also plays a primary role in the health and function of the digital cushion, which is a spongy pad of tissue located at the bottom of the hoof. This cushion acts as a shock absorber, helping dissipate the impact force as the horse moves. Without a proper blood supply, the digital cushion can become damaged, leading to conditions such as navicular syndrome.

The distal limb of a horse, which includes the foot, is rich in blood vessels critical to the health and function of the hoof and other tissues. The prominent veins in the distal limb include the digital vein, which runs along the back of the pastern and carries blood back to the heart, and the digital artery, which runs along the back of the pastern and carries oxygenated blood to the hoof.

The arterial supply to the hoof is provided by the circumflex artery, which branches from the digital artery. This artery is responsible for delivering oxygenated blood to the sensitive laminar tissue of the hoof. The digital veins drain the foot's blood back to the heart.

In addition to the major veins and arteries, the distal limb also contains a network of smaller vessels, including capillaries and venules, that

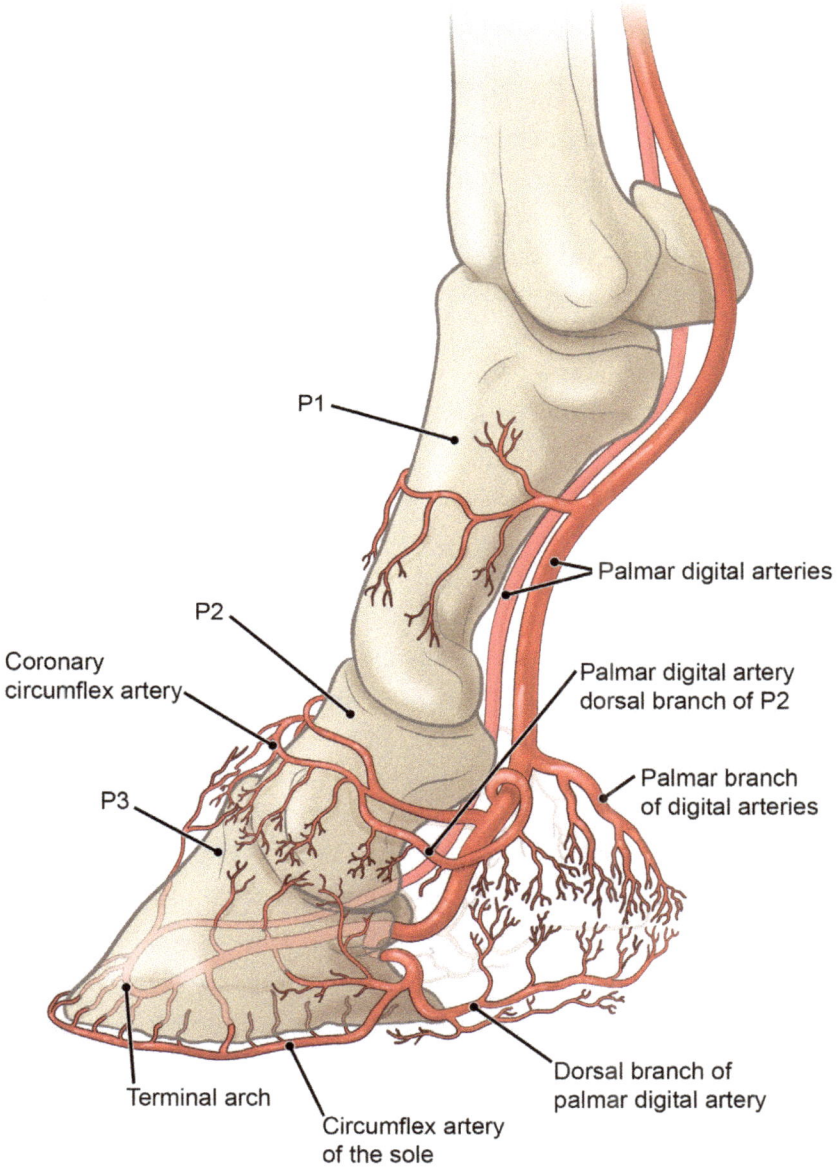

P1

Palmar digital arteries

P2

Coronary
circumflex artery

Palmar digital artery
dorsal branch of P2

P3

Palmar branch
of digital arteries

Terminal arch

Dorsal branch of
palmar digital artery

Circumflex artery
of the sole

help to ensure proper blood flow and oxygenation to the hoof and other tissues. The blood vessels in the distal limb are surrounded by supportive connective tissue and protected by the limb's bones and other structures.

The vasculature of the distal limb of a horse is a complex and critical system that plays a vital role in the health and function of the hoof and other tissues. Horse owners should be aware of the importance of maintaining proper blood flow and oxygenation to the foot and take measures to ensure that their horse's blood vessels are functioning correctly. Any disruption to the blood supply can lead to various hoof problems and conditions, making it extremely important for horse owners to understand the importance of blood supply and to take steps to maintain proper blood flow to the hoof.

The hoof's blood supply plays a crucial role in maintaining hoof health. Here's an overview of the physiology of the hoof's blood supply and how it relates to hoof health:

- **Blood Supply:** The hoof receives its blood supply from the digital artery, which runs along the back of the leg and supplies blood to the foot via the circumflex artery. The blood supply to the hoof is vital for the growth and repair of the hoof and for maintaining proper hoof shape and balance. The hoof wall, or the laminar tissue, is supplied by the laminar blood vessels. These blood vessels run through the hoof wall and provide the necessary nutrients for the growth and repair of the hoof. If the blood supply to the hoof wall is compromised, it can lead to hoof problems such as laminitis, in which the laminar tissue becomes inflamed and can lead to lameness.

- **Digital Cushion:** The circulation in hoof is supplied by the digital cushion, a thick pad of fibrous tissue located at the back of the hoof. The digital cushion helps to maintain healthy circulation in the hoof and provides shock absorption when the horse's foot strikes the ground. It also plays a role in maintaining proper hoof shape and balance.

- **Importance of Proper Blood Flow:** Proper blood flow is essential for maintaining hoof health. When the blood flow to the hoof is restricted, it can lead to problems such as poor hoof growth, poor hoof quality, and a higher risk of hoof injuries or infections. Severe restrictions can even lead to necrosis, the death of tissues and bones.

- **Factors that can affect blood flow:** Several factors can affect blood flow to the hoof, such as poor nutrition, lack of exercise, and poor hoof care. Certain medical conditions, such as laminitis and navicular disease, can also affect blood flow to the hoof. It is essential to keep an eye on the horse's overall health and address any underlying issues impacting their hoof health.

- **Maintaining Proper Blood Flow:** There are several ways to maintain proper blood flow to the hoof. Regular exercise, adequate nutrition, and hoof care are crucial in maintaining good blood flow to the foot. Additionally, working closely with a farrier and monitoring the horse's overall health can help identify and address any issues impacting blood flow to the hoof.

- **Importance of Hoof Trimming and Shoeing:** Regular hoof trimming and shoeing can play a role in maintaining proper blood flow to the hoof. Hoof trimming helps to remove any excess or overgrown hoof tissue, which can restrict blood flow to the foot. Shoeing, when done correctly, can also help to redistribute weight and pressure on the hoof and can help to maintain proper blood flow by reducing constrictions and stimulating the digital cushion.

Conformation

When it comes to hoof care, one size does not fit all. Every horse is different and requires individualized attention to ensure that their hooves are healthy and functioning correctly. Hoof conformations can vary greatly from horse to horse. Some horses may have high, upright hooves, while others may have low, flat hooves. Some horses may have wide and round hooves, while others may have narrow and pointed hooves. These unique conformations are often a result of genetics but can also be influenced by environment and management practices. A farrier must consider your horse's individual hooves to provide the proper balance that ensures its bones, joints, and soft tissues are supported and in optimal alignment.

Hooves that are out of balance or have an abnormal shape can cause pain and lameness and lead to severe problems such as navicular syndrome and soft tissue injuries. Working closely with a farrier and veterinarian can help you to understand your horse's unique hoof conformations and develop a customized hoof care plan that addresses your horse's specific needs.

The rate of growth can also affect the hoof shape and balance. A faster growth rate can cause the hoof to become elongated and can lead to an imbalance in the hoof shape. A slower growth rate can cause the foot to become shortened and can also lead to imbalances.

Different types of hooves may affect hoof health and require special care, for example:

- **Club Foot:** Club foot is characterized by a very steep angle of the hoof wall. The heel is very high, the toe often dished, and there may be bulging at the coronet band. Club foot can vary in severity and some horses can maintain soundness with proper shoeing and care. In more extreme cases, weight bearing is painful and the horse will always be lame.

- **High-Low:** High-low conformation in horses refers to a condition where one or more hooves are longer or shorter than the others. One foot may have a very low, flat angle while the other foot is more upright. This can lead to uneven wear on the hooves, an imbalance in how the horse carries its weight, and an increased risk of injuries. Various factors, such as genetics, inadequate exercise, and improper hoof care, can cause high-low conformation. To address high-low conformation, it is important to consult a veterinarian and farrier to determine the cause and develop a treatment plan. This may include regular hoof trimming and shoeing, changes to the horse's diet, and exercises to improve the horse's balance and muscle strength.

- **Under-Run:** An under-run heel is characterized by a heel angle that is too low in relation to the toe, crushed, and migrated forward. This hoof conformation can lead to problems such as poor weight distribution, increased risk of injury, and difficulty maintaining proper hoof balance. Under-run horses may require special shoeing or trimming to redistribute weight and provide support to the heel.

- **Long Toe, Low Heel:** This hoof conformation is characterized by a longer toe and a lower heel than what is considered ideal. This can lead to an increased risk of injury, poor weight distribution, and difficulty maintaining proper hoof balance. Long-toed, low-heeled horses may require special shoeing or trimming to redistribute weight and support the heel.

- **Flat Feet:** Flat feet have a very low arch and little to no heel. This conformation can lead to an increased risk of injury, poor weight distribution, and difficulty in maintaining proper hoof balance. Flat-footed horses may require special shoeing or trimming to redistribute weight and relieve sole pressure.

Other abnormalities in the horse's overall conformation can affect a horse's health and performance. Some common conformational faults include:

- **Base-narrow or base-wide:** This refers to the width of the horse's foot placement in relation to the width of its body. A base-narrow horse will have its feet closer together than ideal, which can cause uneven weight distribution to the outside aspect of its hoof and limb. A base-wide horse will have a wide stance, which can result in excessive weight distribution to the inside aspect of its hoof.

- **Toed-in or toed-out:** This refers to the alignment of the horse's hooves. A horse that is toed-in, or pigeon-toed, will have hooves that point inward, which can cause uneven wear on the feet. A horse that is toed-out, or splay-footed, will have hooves that point outward. These issues originate from a deviation of the fetlock joint.

- **Weak pasterns:** This refers to a horse with pasterns that are too long or too short, which can cause strain on the tendons and ligaments and lead to lameness. Long, sloping pasterns can put more strain on tendons and ligaments, while short, upright pasterns may be more prone to arthritis from bone-on-bone friction.

- **Carpus Valgus or Carpus Varus:** Carpus Valgus, or "knock-kneed," is an angular limb deformity where the carpus and lower leg deviates away from the body. Carpus Varus, or "bow-legged," refers to a deviation of the carpus and lower limb inward toward the centerline of the body.

- **Over-at-the-knee or back-at-the-knee:** This refers to a deviation of the horse's knee in relation to its leg. An over-at-the-knee, or "buck-kneed," horse will have a knee that is too far forward in relation to its leg, which can cause strain on the joint. A back-at-the-knee, or "calf-kneed," horse will have a knee that is angled backward, which can also cause strain and difficulty with movement.

- **Cow-hocked:** This refers to the alignment of the horse's hocks. A cow-hocked horse will have hocks that point inward, which can cause strain on the joints and lead to lameness.

- **Short back or long back:** This refers to the length of the horse's spine in relation to its body. A short-back horse may have difficulty with balance and mobility, while a long-back horse may be more prone to back problems.

- **Roached or swaybacked:** This refers to the shape of the horse's back. A swaybacked horse will have a back that is too curved, which can cause difficulty with balance and mobility. A roached horse will have a back that is too straight, which can cause movement problems and back pain.

It's worth noting that while these conformational abnormalities can have an impact on the horse's movement and performance, they are not always necessarily problematic. Many horses with minor conformational imperfections have successful careers in various disciplines. Many conformational challenges can be overcome through proper training, management, and hoof care that addresses a horse's unique condition.

Hoof-Pastern Axis

Proper alignment of the horse's digit (phalanges) and understanding the concept of the hoof-pastern axis (HPA) are another crucial aspect of maintaining the overall health and soundness of the horse's limb.

The hoof-pastern axis is the angle formed by the line of the pastern and the line of the hoof. In a correctly aligned foot, the hoof-pastern axis should form a straight line from the fetlock to the ground. This angle is important because it helps distribute the horse's weight evenly across the hoof and helps to absorb shock as the horse moves. An incorrect hoof-pastern axis can place increased stress on joints and soft tissue, leading to various lameness issues and pain in the horse.

A horse's hoof-pastern axis can be affected by various factors, including genetics, conformation, and environment. Some horses may be born with a hoof-pastern axis that is not straight, while others may develop an incorrect axis due to poor hoof care or improper shoeing.

When examining a horse's hoof-pastern axis, it is important to look at the horse from the side and from the front. From the side, the hoof and pastern bones should be in direct alignment from the fetlock to the

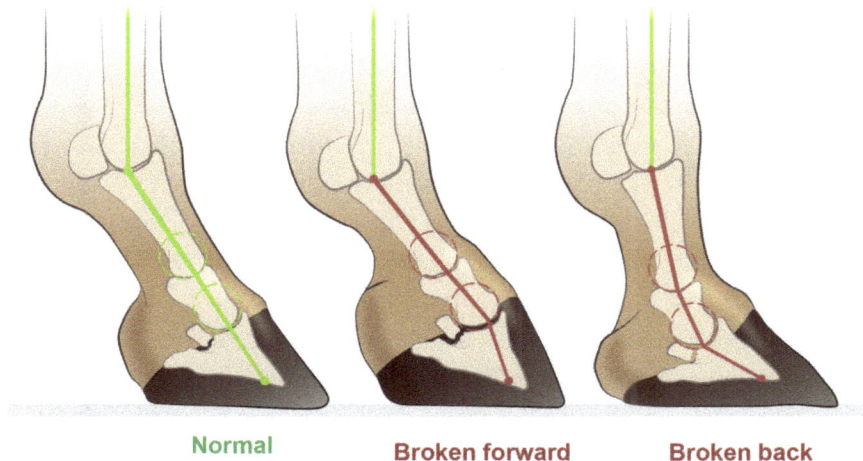

Normal   **Broken forward**   **Broken back**

ground. From the front, the hoof should appear to be centered under the cannon bone, and the pastern should not deviate in either direction.

The hoof-pastern axis is a crucial aspect of maintaining the overall health and soundness of a horse's limb. Incorrect angles in this area of the limb can cause excessive strain on tendons and ligaments, leading to more complicated injuries. A digit that is out of alignment can also result in damage to the bones and joints and be a precursor to arthritic conditions. Proper hoof care, including regular trims and shoeing, as well as addressing any issues with the hoof-pastern axis through corrective shoeing or hoof modification, can help prevent lameness and pain in the horse.

A horse with a "broken-back" hoof pattern axis has a pastern that is more upright than the hoof. This type of alignment can cause increased stress on the tendons and ligaments in the lower leg, as well as increased stress on the DIP (distal interphalangeal)joint. It can also cause problems such as arthritis, and navicular disease.

A horse with a "broken-forward" hoof pattern axis has a hoof that is more upright than the pastern. This means that the angle formed between the foot and the pastern is larger than it should be. This type of alignment can cause increased stress on the tendons and ligaments in the lower leg, particularly the suspensory ligament. It can also cause problems such as arthritis and lower limb lameness.

Proper hoof-pastern alignment is essential for optimal horse health and performance. The structures of the horses limb, the bones and tendons, have developed to support the horse's immense weight. When these structures are out of alignment, leverage and extreme forces can cause injuries in one or more parts of the horse.

Corrective shoeing may be able to improve a broken-back or broken-forward HPA. A professional farrier should be consulted to determine the best course of action. In some cases, hoof imbalances may also be corrected through hoof trimming and reshaping by a professional farrier or equine podiatrist.

Not all horses will have perfect hoof-pastern alignment, and it can also vary from one foot to another. Therefore it is important to have a professional farrier or veterinarian evaluate the horse's hoof-pastern axis on a regular basis to ensure that the horse remains comfortable and sound.

Leverage & Breakover

Leverage is a mechanical advantage that helps to create force or movement. There are three main components of leverage in a horse: the head, neck, and legs. The head and neck can be thought of as the lever arm, the point of balance is the center of gravity, and the legs act as the fulcrum. When a horse moves, the head and neck are moved in a specific direction to create the desired movement. The legs then use this movement to create leverage and push the horse forward.

For example, when a horse is asked to move forward, the rider will typically ask the horse to raise its head and neck. This movement shifts the center of gravity to the rear and distributes more weight to the hind legs. The hind legs then push off the ground to create forward momentum. This is an example of how the principles of leverage can be used to create movement.

It is important to consider the principles of leverage when working with a horse, as an imbalance in the horse's head and neck can have

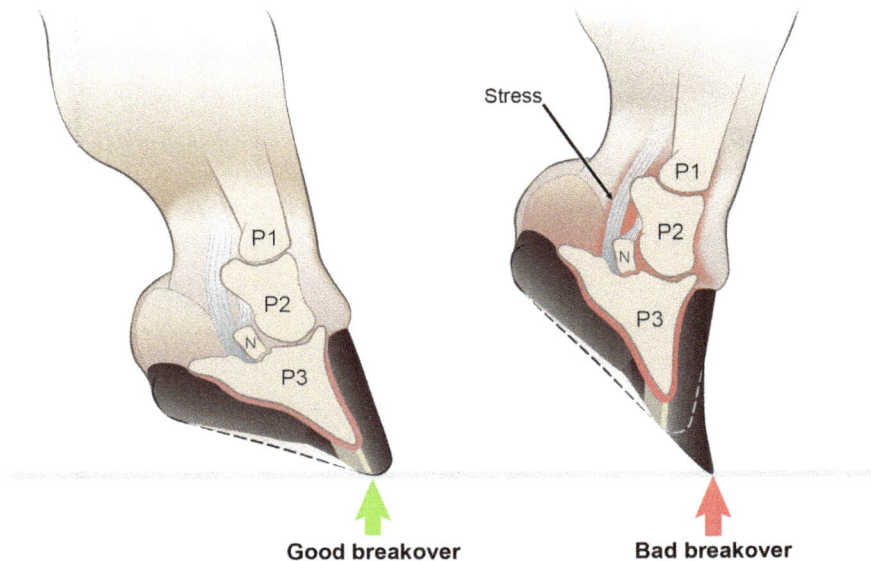

Good breakover

Bad breakover

negative effects on the horse's movement and overall health. If the head and neck are positioned too far downward, it can put undue strain on the horse's back and spine, leading to discomfort and potentially causing long-term damage. Conversely, if the head and neck are positioned too far back, it can limit the horse's ability to balance and move effectively.

The principles of leverage have a significant impact on a horse's limbs and understanding them can be helpful in identifying and correcting common movement problems in horses, such as lack of engagement, stiffness, and resistance. By working to improve the horse's balance and overall posture, horse owners can help to improve the horse's performance, reduce the risk of injury, and maintain the horse's overall health and well-being.

The basic principle of leverage refers to the force that is created by the position of an object, such as a horse's limb. In horses, the lower leg is the lever, and the foot is the load. The position of the hoof relative to the cannon bone creates a torque that is either favorable or unfavorable to the limb. When the hoof is correctly positioned under the limb, the force of impact is absorbed by the bones, tendons, and ligaments, which helps distribute the weight and reduce stress.

When the hoof is not correctly positioned under the limb, the forces generated by the hoof can cause imbalances and stress to the limb. For example, when the hoof is too far forward, the lever becomes too long, which increases the force placed on the limb. Conversely, when the hoof is too far back, the lever becomes too short, which reduces the ability of the limb to absorb force.

In horses, the hoof should be correctly positioned so that the center of the foot is directly beneath the coffin joint. This helps create a balanced load that reduces stress on the limb and helps maintain proper limb alignment. If the hoof is not correctly positioned, it can lead to issues such as navicular syndrome, joint problems, and arthritis.

Another aspect of leverage that affects a horse's limbs is the angle of the pastern. The angle of the pastern is critical to the health of the limb because it affects the forces that are transmitted through the limb. A horse with a steep, upright pastern angle will exert more forces through its bones and joints, reducing its ability to absorb impact, and may be

more likely to develop arthritic conditions. Conversely, a horse with a long, sloping pastern will generate less force through the limb and rely more heavily on the strength of tendons and ligaments. A horse with long, sloping pasterns may provide a smoother ride, but will be more susceptible to soft tissue injuries.

The principles of leverage are also an important concept in the understanding of how a horse's hooves function. A horse's hoof is a complex structure that provides support, shock absorption, and propulsion for the animal. The hoof wall, frog, and digital cushion work together to form the lever system that allows the horse to move efficiently and with balance.

The principles of leverage state that the position of the fulcrum (the point at which a lever rotates) determines the effectiveness of the lever. In the case of the horse's hoof, the fulcrum is located at the level of the coffin joint, which is the joint that connects the hoof to the rest of the leg.

When the hoof is balanced and the fulcrum is located in the correct position, the lever system is able to effectively absorb shock and provide stability. However, when the hoof is unbalanced or the fulcrum is positioned incorrectly, the lever system is less effective and can result in a variety of problems, such as lameness, hoof pain, and decreased performance.

A horse's hoof can become unbalanced or have an incorrect fulcrum position due to a variety of factors, including conformation, injury, improper toe length and shoeing practices. For example, a horse with a broken-forward or broken-back hoof pastern axis may have a hoof that is unbalanced and puts excessive stress on the lever system, resulting in pain and lameness.

Breakover is a term used to describe the point in time during a horse's stride where the foot leaves the ground and begins to move forward. This is a critical point in a horse's gait and can have significant effects on the horse's comfort, soundness, and performance. Understanding the meaning and importance of breakover is important for horse owners and caretakers to ensure the well-being and health of their horses.

Breakover can be considered as a physical point on the hoof where the foot levers off of the ground, as well as referring to the length of time that the hoof in motion is in contact with the ground and the ease with which it can be lifted off the ground. This is affected by several factors, including the length and angle of the horse's bones and tendons in the lower limb, the angle and shape of the hoof, and the weight and balance of the horse. If the breakover is too far forward, the horse may have trouble lifting its foot and can suffer from chronic pain or lameness. If the breakover is too short, the horse may have trouble balancing and may be prone to tripping or stumbling.

In order to achieve an optimal breakover, several factors must be considered when evaluating the health and soundness of a horse's hooves. This includes the overall shape and angle of the hoof, the position of the bones inside the hoof, the length of the horse's bones and stress on tendons, as well as the overall balance and weight distribution of the horse. A veterinarian or farrier can assist in evaluating these factors and making recommendations for hoof care, including trimming and shoeing, to optimize breakover and ensure the comfort and health of the horse.

Farriery

THROUGHOUT THE TIME HUMANS HAVE domesticated horses, people have been finding ways to care for their hooves. Trimming and shoeing horses can be traced back to ancient civilizations such as the Egyptians and Greeks. These early horse caretakers recognized the importance of maintaining the health of a horse's hooves to keep the animal sound and able to work.

In the early days of horse domestication, horses were primarily used for transportation and farming. Their hooves were trimmed and shaped to fit the terrain in which they worked. For example, horses living in rocky or mountainous regions had hooves trimmed and shaped to grip the uneven ground better. In contrast, horses living in flat and sandy areas had hooves trimmed and shaped to distribute their weight better and prevent them from sinking into the ground.

As horses were used for different purposes, farriers began to experiment with different types of shoes. The earliest known horseshoes were made of bronze and were used by the ancient Celts. These shoes were designed to protect the horse's hooves from wear and tear and to provide better traction on slippery surfaces. In other areas, horses' hooves my have been protected by leather boots or pads of tightly woven reeds.

Over time, farriers began to experiment with different materials and designs for horseshoes. The Roman hipposandal was an iron boot that could be temporarily attached to a horse's hoof with metal clips and leather straps. Iron and steel shoes became popular in the Middle Ages as they were more durable than bronze shoes. Farriers used these shoes to support horses that worked on hard surfaces.

In the 20th century, farriers began to use aluminum and plastic shoes. These materials were lightweight and provided good traction on a variety of surfaces. They also helped to reduce the weight on the horse's hooves, which helped to prevent injuries and lameness.

Today, farriers continue to use a variety of materials and designs for horseshoes. They also use different techniques for trimming and shaping hooves, depending on the horse's conformation, the type of work the horse does, and the terrain in which the horse lives.

Overall, the history of trimming and shoeing horses is long and fascinating, full of experimentation and innovation. Today's farriers continue to use the knowledge and techniques developed over the centuries to keep horses' hooves healthy, sound, and able to perform the tasks for which they are used. By understanding the history of hoof care, horse owners can better understand the importance of regular hoof care and the farrier's role in maintaining their horse's health and well-being.

A Farrier's Role

The farrier's role in hoof care is critical for horses' overall health and well-being. A farrier is a trained professionals with specialized knowledge and skills who specializes in caring for and maintaining a horse's hooves. They are responsible for trimming and shoeing the horse's feet and providing advice and guidance on hoof care.

A farrier's responsibilities include:

- **Trimming:** Farriers are responsible for regular hoof trimming, which involves removing excess hoof growth and maintaining the correct shape and balance of the hooves. This helps to redistribute weight and prevent injury. Farriers are trained to understand the hoof's structure and function and to trim the feet to promote proper hoof balance and leverage.

- **Shoeing:** Farriers are also responsible for shoeing horses. They will determine if a horse needs shoeing and, if so, will fit and apply the appropriate type of shoe to the horse's hoof. They will also adjust the shoe as necessary to ensure a good fit and to redistribute weight.

- **Hoof Health Evaluation:** Farriers are trained to evaluate the overall health of the horse's hooves. They will identify any abnormalities or issues that could lead to hoof problems and advise on the best action to take.

- **Advice and guidance:** Farriers are a valuable resource for horse owners, providing advice and guidance on hoof care. They can advise on diet and nutrition, environment and management, and regular hoof care and maintenance.

- **Regular Follow-up:** Farriers are responsible for regular follow-up on their client's horses to ensure that the hooves are healthy and in good condition and to make any necessary adjustments to the horse's trimming or shoeing.

Education & Certification

The education and training of farriers is a long and detailed process that requires a great deal of dedication and hard work. Farriers are skilled professionals who specialize in the care and maintenance of horses' hooves, and they play a vital role in the health and well-being of these animals.

Typically, the first step in becoming a farrier is either to enroll in an 8 week farrier training program, or complete a farrier apprenticeship. Apprenticeships may last between two and four years and provide hands-on training under the guidance of a skilled and experienced farrier. During this time, apprentices learn the basics of hoof anatomy and physiology and how to trim and shoe horses properly. They also learn how to use the tools of the trade, such as hammers, nippers, and rasps.

After completing an apprenticeship, many farriers continue their education by taking courses and attending workshops to learn new techniques and stay current with the latest advancements in the field.

Interested farriers can take these courses through professional organizations such as the American Farrier's Association or the British Farrier's Association.

In addition to education and training, farriers may also pass a certification exam. Professional organizations typically administer certification exams and cover hoof anatomy, trimming and shoeing techniques, and business management.

Becoming a farrier requires a great deal of dedication and hard work. However, for those passionate about horse care and willing to invest the time and effort, a career as a farrier can be both rewarding and fulfilling. With their expertise and knowledge, farriers play an essential role in ensuring horses' health and well-being and helping horse owners provide the best possible care for their animals.

Professional Organizations & Continued Education

Farriery is a highly skilled trade that requires a great deal of education and training. As such, there are many professional organizations that farriers may choose to belong to in order to further their education, stay up to date on the latest techniques and technologies, and network with other farriers.

In the United States, several professional organizations for farriers aim to promote and improve the standard of farriery practice and education. Some of the most notable organizations include:

- **American Farrier's Association (AFA):** This is the largest farrier organization in the United States and has existed since 1978. The AFA offers its members a wide range of services, including education, certification, and networking opportunities. They also host an annual convention, the largest gathering of farriers in the world, and hold regular clinics and workshops.

- **The International/American Association of Professional Farriers (IAPF/AAPF):** This organization aims to promote farriers' education and professional development. They offer a certification program and hold an annual convention, as well as regular clinics and workshops.

- **The Equine Lameness Prevention Organization (ELPO):** This organization focuses on education and lameness prevention and management. They operate a full farrier school, certification programs and regular clinics.

- **The Brotherhood of Working Farriers Association (BWFA):** This organization is focused on promoting the education and professional development of farriers who work primarily with performance horses. They hold an annual conference and regular clinics and workshops.

These are just a few examples of the professional organizations that exist to support farriers and promote the highest standards of farriery practice. Joining one of these organizations can be an excellent way for farriers to stay informed about the latest developments in the field, network with other farriers and horse owners, and continue their education.

Finding a Qualified Farrier

When looking for a highly skilled farrier, there are several things that a horse owner should consider. The first step is to ask for recommendations from other horse owners, trainers, or veterinarians in your area. They may have experience with a farrier that they trust and can recommend.

Another important consideration is the farrier's level of education and experience. A highly skilled farrier typically has completed a training program and may have passed a certification exam. They will also continue to educate themselves through ongoing continuing education classes and workshops. Additionally, it's essential to ask about the farrier's experience working with different types of horses and any specialties or areas of expertise they may have.

Certification exams, or other educational opportunities, may allow the farrier to attach certain letters to their name. You may see CF, CPF, CJF, AF, APF, or numerous other initials following their name. A farrier without any of these letters is <u>not</u> an indicator that you will receive poor quality work. A farrier without these extra initials may be very knowledgeable, competent, and highly skilled. These letters merely indicate that the farrier has met a prescribed criteria, passed a test, or is dedicated to receiving continued education.

When hiring a farrier, it's also important to consider the horse's needs and any specific issues it may have. For example, if your horse has a history of lameness or other hoof problems, you'll want to look for a farrier who has experience treating those issues.

Finally, it's essential to establish a good working relationship with your farrier. Clear communication, regular check-ins, and a good understanding of your horse's needs and goals will help to ensure that your horse's hooves are well cared for. Overall, finding a highly skilled farrier takes time and research, but ensuring that your horse's hooves are healthy and well-maintained is crucial.

Farrier-Client Relationship

When you establish a relationship with your farrier, you can be sure that your horse's hooves are in the best possible condition. A farrier is a highly skilled professional responsible for caring for and maintaining your horse's hooves. They are trained to understand the intricacies of hoof anatomy, physiology, and shoeing, and they can provide valuable insights and recommendations on how to best care for your horse's feet.

You can establish and maintain a positive, productive relationship with your farrier, ensuring that your horse receives the best possible care for their hooves. Here are some key considerations for building and maintaining a positive relationship with your farrier:

- **Communication:** Maintaining clear and open communication with your farrier is essential for understanding your horse's hoof care needs and ensuring they are met. Be sure to share any concerns or observations you have about your horse's hooves with your farrier, and ask any questions you may have about the care and maintenance of your horse's hooves.

- **Trust:** Trust is a critical component of any professional relationship, and it is imperative to care for your horse. Look for a farrier who is knowledgeable, experienced, and has a good reputation within the equine community.

- **Scheduling:** Regular hoof care is essential for maintaining the health and well-being of your horse. Establishing a regular schedule for trims and shoeing can prevent lameness and injury, as well as potentially expensive veterinary bills. Work with your farrier to develop a program that works for both of you, and make sure to communicate any changes or cancellations as soon as possible.

- **Payment:** Discuss the payment terms with your farrier and make sure you understand the costs of services and materials. A good farrier will be upfront about the price and provide you with an invoice for the work done.

- **Safety:** Safety is of the utmost importance when working with horses. Make sure your farrier has insurance and follow safety guidelines when your farrier is working with your horse.

- **Flexibility:** Be open to suggestions from your farrier, as they may have knowledge and expertise that you lack. Your farrier may recommend a different shoeing or trimming technique that could benefit your horse's hooves.

- **Respect:** Show your farrier respect by being on time for appointments and keeping your horse clean and groomed. Your farrier will appreciate it, and it will make their job easier.

- **Feedback:** Provide constructive feedback to your farrier, both positive and negative. This will help them improve their services and help you be more satisfied with their work.

The Farrier's Goal

A farrier's goal in trimming a horse's hooves is to maintain a healthy, functional hoof that will allow the horse to move comfortably and efficiently, reducing the risk of injury and improving overall performance and wellbeing. This involves a combination of both art and science, as each horse's hoof will be unique and may require slightly different approaches based on factors such as conformation, age, activity level, and living conditions. The following are some of the key considerations when trimming a horse's hooves:

- **Maintaining proper hoof length:** The hoof should be trimmed to a length that allows the horse to maintain its natural breakover point, which is the point at which the front of the hoof leaves the ground during movement. Hooves that are too long can cause discomfort and impede the horse's ability to move efficiently, while hooves that are trimmed too short can put added stress on the horse's limb joints and tendons.

- **Balancing the hoof capsule:** The hoof should be trimmed to balance the hoof capsule, ensuring that the hoof is balanced from side to side and front to back, evenly around the coffin bone. This will help to distribute weight across the hoof and prevent any one area from becoming overstressed due to leverage.

- **Removing excessive sole thickness:** The sole should be trimmed to a thickness that allows the horse to feel the ground and maintain good footing, but is not so thick as to impede circulation or become a breeding ground for bacteria.

- **Heel placement:** The heel should be trimmed to a length that allows for good shock absorption, but not so long that it interferes with the horse's movement or puts excessive stress on the heel.

- **Maintaining the frog:** The frog should be trimmed to maintain its natural shape and function as a shock absorber and pump for the circulatory system. The sides of the frog should be neatly trimmed to promote natural cleaning and prevent build-up of dirt and manure.

- **Maintaining proper angles:** The angles of the hoof should be maintained at the correct proportions to allow for proper biomechanics during movement. This includes the angle of the hoof wall, the angle of the sole, and the angle between the hoof wall and the pastern. Note that these angles are proportional and should be determined for the particular horse and even individual hooves. Fifty-one degrees may be perfect for your neighbor's horse, but maybe not for yours.

Barefoot or Shod?

Leaving a horse barefoot, or without the use of horseshoes, is becoming an increasingly popular choice among horse owners. Going barefoot has several benefits, both for the horse and the owner.

One of the main benefits of barefoot horses is that they have a better chance of maintaining healthy hooves. Horseshoes can interfere with the natural growth and wear of the hoof, leading to issues such as cracks, chips, and overgrown hooves. When a horse is barefoot, their feet are free to grow and wear naturally, which helps to keep them strong and healthy.

Another benefit of barefoot horses is that they can better feel and respond to the terrain they are on. When a horse has shoes on, it may not be able to feel the ground as well, which can make them less responsive and more prone to injury. Barefoot horses can feel the ground beneath them, which allows them to adjust their gait and footing, making them less likely to slip or stumble.

Barefoot horses may also have a reduced risk of developing problems with their tendons and ligaments. Horseshoes can change how a horse's hoof hits the ground, and improperly applied shoes can put extra stress on the tendons and ligaments in the horse's legs. When a horse is barefoot, their hooves can hit the ground more naturally, reducing the risk of injury to these structures.

Horseshoes wear out and need to be replaced, which can be costly and time-consuming for the owner. Additionally, with the constant wear and tear on the hooves from applying and removing shoes, the horse may develop hoof problems that require more specialized care.

Additionally, barefoot horses can be less expensive to maintain long-term, as there are no shoeing costs or costs associated with maintaining shoes.

It is important to note that the transition to barefoot from shod should be done gradually and with the guidance of a farrier or veterinarian to avoid any discomfort or injury to the horse. It is also essential to provide good hoof care and regular trimmings to ensure that the horse's hooves are healthy and strong enough to go barefoot.

When deciding whether to leave a horse barefoot or use horseshoes, there are several factors to consider:

First, consider the horse's unique conformation and hoof structure. Some horses naturally have strong, healthy hooves that may not require additional support from horseshoes, while others may have weaker feet that may benefit from the added support. A veterinarian or farrier can help determine a specific horse's best course of action.

Second, consider the horse's living conditions and use. Horses primarily kept in a pasture and used for light riding may not need shoes. In contrast, horses used for heavy work or competition may benefit from the added support and protection provided by horseshoes.

Third, it is important to consider the terrain and conditions in which the horse will be ridden or worked. Horses that will be ridden on hard, rocky terrain may benefit from shoes, while horses that will be ridden on soft, grassy terrain may not need them.

Fourth, calculate the cost and maintenance required for shoeing versus leaving your horse barefoot. Horseshoeing needs to be done regularly and can be costly in the long run. While going barefoot may save on shoeing costs, it may increase the need for regular hoof trims and care.

Ultimately, the decision to leave a horse barefoot or use horseshoes should be based on the horse's individual needs and the owner's goals for the horse. Working closely with a veterinarian and farrier is essential to make an informed decision.

Consideration of Horseshoes

Historically, horses have been used for various purposes, such as transportation, agriculture, and warfare. As human civilization has progressed, so has the way we utilize and care for these majestic animals. One aspect of horse care that has seen significant evolution is the use of horseshoes.

The earliest known evidence of horseshoes dates back to around the first century AD in what is now modern-day France. These early horseshoes were made of metal and were designed to protect the horse's hooves from wear and tear on hard surfaces. They were also used to help horses navigate through soft or wet terrain. It is likely that people were protecting their horse's hooves by other means much before this.

As time passed, horseshoes became more advanced and specialized. The rise of the nail-on horseshoe by the 6th or 7th century allowed for a more secure fit and greater durability. The use of different materials such as iron, steel, and even gold and silver became popular as the technology to make them improved.

During the Middle Ages, blacksmiths began developing specialized horseshoes for different purposes. For example, specialized horseshoes were used for warhorses to provide extra protection and grip in battle.

Horseshoes with a lighter design were used for racing horses to allow for more speed.

As the Industrial Revolution took hold in the 18th and 19th centuries, the production of horseshoes became more efficient and standardized. The steam-powered hammer's invention allowed the mass production of horseshoes and made them more affordable for horse owners.

Today, horseshoes continue to evolve and be refined. Modern horseshoes are made from various materials, including aluminum and plastic, and are designed for specific activities such as show jumping, dressage, and endurance racing. Additionally, glue-on horseshoes have become increasingly popular as they provide a more secure fit and can be used for a longer period of time than traditional nail-on shoes.

There are several reasons why a horse might need to be shod rather than left barefoot. Primarily, we will shoe a horse for protection, traction, or correction. Some considerations include the horse's intended use, the condition of the horse's hooves, and the environment in which the horse will be living and working.

First and foremost, the horse's intended use is an important consideration. Horses participating in high-impact activities such as jumping, dressage, and racing will likely require shoes to protect their hooves and provide the necessary traction for these activities. Additionally, horses working on hard surfaces such as concrete or asphalt may need shoes to protect their feet from wear and injury.

Another important consideration is the condition of the horse's hooves. Horses with poor hoof quality, such as those with thin or weak hooves, may need shoes to protect their feet and improve their overall hoof health. Additionally, horses with certain hoof conditions, such as navicular syndrome, may require shoes to provide additional support and alleviate pain.

Finally, you must also consider the environment in which the horse will live and work. Horses living in wet or muddy environments may need shoes to protect their hooves from becoming overgrown or infected. Additionally, horses living in rocky or uneven terrain may need shoes to protect their feet from injury and provide additional traction.

While many horses may be able to go barefoot, some will require shoes to protect and support their overall hoof health. Factors such as

intended use, hoof condition, and environment must all be considered when deciding whether to shoe a horse. It is always best to consult with a veterinarian and farrier to make the best decision for the horse.

Uses of Horseshoes

Horseshoes can influence a horse's gait by altering how weight is distributed on the hoof and providing support to the foot and lower limb. The type and design of the shoe, as well as the way it is applied, can affect the horse's gait.

For example, certain types of shoes, such as rocker or bar shoes, can help relieve heel pressure and promote a more natural breakover. This can help reduce heel stress and promote a more comfortable, efficient gait.

Other types of shoes, such as wedged shoes, can help balance the hoof and promote a more level gait. Wedged shoes can correct imbalances in the foot, such as underrun heels, and can help promote a more comfortable and efficient gait.

In addition, certain types of therapeutic shoes can be used to support the hoof and lower limb. These shoes can help manage conditions such as navicular syndrome, laminitis, or chronic foot pain.

It is important to note that the use of shoes should be guided by the horse's individual needs and should be based on a thorough examination of the horse's conformation, hoof shape, and gait. It is also essential to work closely with a farrier and veterinarian to ensure that the shoeing plan is appropriate for the horse's needs and will benefit its overall health.

Horseshoes can influence a horse's gait by adjusting the shape and position of the shoe to alter the way the horse's foot strikes the ground. This can be done to address specific gait abnormalities, such as a short stride or overreaching, or to enhance a horse's performance within a particular discipline.

In some cases, farriers may also use therapeutic shoes to address specific gait abnormalities. For example, a shoe with a rocker bottom can address a horse with a short stride or overreaching. Or, a shoe with a built-up heel can manage a horse with a contracted heel.

It's important to note that these adjustments must be made by a skilled farrier who has been trained in the specific techniques and should be done with the guidance of a veterinarian. Every horse is unique and requires an individualized approach.

Horseshoes can treat various hoof disorders by providing support and protection to the affected area. Some examples include:

- **Laminitis:** Horseshoes can be used to redistribute weight and take pressure off the affected area by using shoes with a particular design, such as heart-bar shoes or egg-bar shoes.

- **Navicular syndrome:** A modified horseshoe design, such as a rolled toe or a wedge pad, can provide additional support for the heel and reduce the stress on the navicular bone.

- **Hoof abscesses:** Horseshoes can protect the affected area and provide support while the horse is healing.

- **Ringbone and sidebone:** Using horseshoes with a particular design, such as a raised heel or a rocker toe, can reduce the stress on the affected joint.

- **Hoof cracks:** Special shoes, like full support or heart-bar shoes, can protect the affected area and provide additional support.

- **Hoof injuries:** Horses with certain hoof injuries can benefit from the unique design of a glue-on or bar shoe, which offers protection for the affected area and provides support during the healing process.

It is important to note that while horseshoes can be used to treat hoof disorders, they are not a substitute for proper care, management, and veterinary attention. The use of horseshoes should be decided by a veterinarian or a farrier, who will consider the horse's individual case, breed, age, and activity level, among other factors.

There are many different types of horseshoes available for different purposes and uses. Regular shoes are the most common type of horseshoe and are used to protect the horse's hooves from wear and tear and to provide traction on hard surfaces. They are typically made of steel or aluminum and come in a variety of sizes and shapes to fit different hoof shapes and sizes.

Therapeutic horseshoes are designed to provide support and protection for horses with specific hoof conditions or injuries. Therapeutic shoes help horses with specific hoof conditions such as laminitis, navicular syndrome, or chronic foot pain. These shoes often have special features such as elevated heels or modified toe shapes to help redistribute weight and reduce stress on the affected areas. They may also be made of rubber or plastic to provide additional support and cushioning. It's important to note that therapeutic shoes should only be used under a veterinarian's or farrier's guidance, as improper use can cause further harm to the horse.

Sport-specific shoes are designed for specific equestrian disciplines such as jumping, dressage, or racing. These shoes often have special features to enhance performance, such as extra traction for jumping or lightweight materials for racing.

In addition to these, there are also different types of horseshoes for different seasons and terrains. For example, studded shoes can be used for icy or slippery surfaces, while snow pads can be added to regular shoes for use in snowy conditions.

Your farrier should be consulted before choosing a type of shoe for your horse, as the wrong shoe may cause more harm than good. A qualified farrier will be able to assess your horses's conformation and peculiarities to recommend an appropriate shoe. Farriers are trained professionals who are well-versed in different types of horseshoes and their uses. They can evaluate the horse's hoof and recommend the best shoe for its needs.

Safety During Hoof Care

Trimming and shoeing a horse can be a challenging task, but with proper preparation and safety measures in place, it can be done safely and effectively. By taking the necessary precautions and being mindful of the potential risks, horse owners and farriers can ensure that the trimming and shoeing process is as safe and stress-free as possible for the horse.

First and foremost, ensuring that the horse is adequately restrained while receiving hoof care is important. Ideally, a horse should be well-trained to stand calmly for the procedure. A trained horse may be held in cross-ties or tied to a post by its lead rope. If the horse is not able to stand quietly, then a restraint should be employed to ensure the safety of the farrier and owner. An unruly horse can be restrained in stocks or be sedated by a veterinarian. It can also be helpful to have a second person present to assist in holding the horse. This person should be able to quickly release the horse in an emergency.

Another crucial safety aspect during a hoof care procedure is understanding the horse's body language. An anxious or uncomfortable horse often shows signs such as pinned ears, a swishing tail, or a tense body. It is vital to recognize these signs and take appropriate action, such as stopping the procedure and allowing the horse to rest and calm down before continuing. Do not allow the horse to become so agitated that it becomes a danger to the farrier.

Horses can also be prone to certain health conditions affecting the trimming and shoeing process. Laminitis, for example, is a condition that affects the sensitive laminar tissue within the hoof, making it particularly painful for the horse to stand. A horse in extreme pain will have difficulty standing with one foot off the ground for an extended time necessary for trimming. It is important to be aware of any pre-existing conditions and to communicate any issues with the farrier in order to take the necessary precautions.

When providing hoof care to your horse, it is essential to ensure the environment is safe to prevent accidents or injuries to you, the farrier and the horse. Here are some key considerations to keep in mind:

- **Clear the area:** Before beginning any hoof care procedure, make sure the area is clear of any obstacles or debris that could cause a tripping hazard for a person or your horse. This includes removing any sharp objects or tools that could be kicked or stepped on.

- **Firm footing:** Even a calm and trained horse may pull its leg or shift its weight occasionally. The area designated for hoof care and grooming should be flat and level ground with firm footing to avoid falls. Flat and level ground is also necessary for the farrier to accurately assess minute details of the horse's conformation.

- **Good lighting:** If trimming a shoeing will take place inside the barn, make sure to provide adequate lighting. Impaired visibility can be dangerous for you, the farrier, and the horse.

- **No traps:** Be aware and do not allow yourself to be caught between the horse and a wall. Always have an escape route in case the horse becomes agitated and be aware that you're not blocking someone else's escape. Likewise, be cautious that your hands and fingers don't get caught in any tack or rope.

- **Be aware of the horse's behavior:** Always pay attention to the horse's behavior and body language. If they become agitated, nervous, or start to move around too much, take a break and give them time to calm down before continuing.

- **Have a plan:** Have a plan in case of an emergency, such as the horse becoming agitated or getting loose. Make sure you have a way to safely contain the horse and call for help if necessary.

- **Have a first aid kit:** Make sure you have a first aid kit on hand in case of an emergency. Keep it well-stocked and easily accessible.

Training for Hoof Care

Properly training a horse to behave during trimming and shoeing is of the utmost importance for both the safety of the horse and the person handling them. A horse that is not trained to stand still and allow its hooves to be handled can cause serious injury or death to itself and those around them.

One of the most significant dangers of not training a horse for hoof care is the risk of the horse kicking or striking out. A horse that is frightened or uncomfortable during hoof care may try to defend itself by lashing out with its legs. This can cause serious injury or death to the person handling the horse and damage to the horse's legs or hooves.

Another danger of not training a horse for hoof care is the risk of the horse becoming stressed or agitated. A horse that is not used to having its hooves handled may become anxious or frightened during the process, which can lead to an increase in heart rate and blood pressure. This can cause health problems for the horse, as well as making it more difficult for the person handling them to trim or shoe their hooves properly.

In addition to the risk of kicking, a horse that is not trained to stand still during hoof care may also try to pull away or move its feet, making it difficult or even impossible for the person handling them to trim or shoe their hooves properly. The area of a horses hoof that can safely receive nails is about two millimeters wide; a very narrow margin for a moving target. This can lead to substandard trimming or shoeing, which can cause long-term damage to the horse's hooves and legs.

Proper hoof care training can also help prevent the development of behavioral issues in the horse. A horse that is trained to stand still and allow its hooves to be handled from a young age is less likely to develop behavioral problems later on. This can make the process of trimming and shoeing much more pleasant for both the horse and the person handling them.

Proper training for hoof care is essential for the safety and well-being of both the horse and the person handling them. A newborn foal should start receiving farrier visits within the first month of its life. By starting training early and using positive reinforcement, horse owners can ensure that their horse is calm and well-behaved during trimming and shoeing, reducing the risk of injury and making the process more pleasant for all involved.

Before beginning any training, it is vital to understand the nature of horses and their natural instincts. Horses are prey animals, which means they have a strong flight response when they feel threatened. This can make it difficult for them to trust and cooperate with humans, especially when handling their feet.

Establishing a routine is the first step in training a horse to stand for trimming and shoeing. This means setting aside specific times of the day or week to work on hoof care and sticking to that schedule. Consistency is key when working with horses, as they thrive on routine and predictability.

Next, creating a safe and comfortable environment for the horse is vital. This means providing a clean and well-lit area with sound footing, and ensuring that all necessary tools and equipment are easily accessible. It is also essential to approach the horse calmly and quietly, as sudden movements or loud noises can startle the animal and make it more challenging to work with.

To begin the training, it is essential to start with basic ground manners. This includes teaching the horse to stand still, lead, and be handled all over its body, including its feet. This can be achieved through positive reinforcement techniques, such as clicker or treat-based training. These techniques help to build trust and positive associations between the horse and the person doing the work.

Once the horse is comfortable with basic ground manners, introduce them to the tools and equipment used in trimming and shoeing. This can include rasps, nippers, stands, and hoof picks. It is important to take the time to familiarize the horse with these tools and to show them that they are not a threat. This can be done by allowing the horse to sniff and investigate the tools and using positive reinforcement when the horse is calm and relaxed.

Once the horse is comfortable with the tools, begin desensitizing it to having its feet handled. This can be done by gradually increasing the amount of handling and manipulation of the feet, starting with just a few seconds at a time and progressively increasing the duration. Use positive reinforcement and take the time to allow the horse to relax and become comfortable with the handling.

As the horse becomes more comfortable with having its feet handled, it is important to begin teaching it specific behaviors that will make trimming and shoeing easier and safer. This training can include standing still, lifting its foot, and holding it in a particular position. These behaviors can be taught using positive reinforcement techniques and breaking down the task into smaller, manageable steps.

Teaching the horse to tolerate the sound and sensation of the tools being used on its hooves is also important. This can be done by gradually exposing the horse to the sound and sensation of the tools, tapping on its feet with a hammer or hoof pick, and using positive reinforcement when the horse remains calm and relaxed.

Teaching the horse to place its foot on a stand or block is also important, as this will make it easier to work on its hooves. You can begin by leading the horse to the stand and allowing it to sniff and inspect it. Once the horse is comfortable with the stand, you can start leading the horse onto it and rewarding it with treats and praise.

As the horse becomes more comfortable with hoof care, you can begin working on more advanced maneuvers such as trimming and shoeing. It is essential to take things slowly and never push the horse beyond its comfort level. If the horse becomes agitated or uncomfortable, stop and take a break.

Finally, it is important to regularly practice and reinforce the behaviors and skills that have been taught. Regular practice will help to maintain the horse's comfort and trust hoof care procedures. It will also help to ensure that the horse is in good condition and that its hooves are healthy.

Training a horse to stand for trimming and shoeing is a necessary process that requires patience, consistency, and a positive approach. While it is helpful to start training a horse at a young age, even older horses can be trained if you are consistent and take your time with the process. With patience and positive reinforcement, most horses can be trained to stand still for hoof care.

It's important to note that, with few exceptions, farriers are not horse trainers. The farriers's job is to trim and shoe your horse, not teach it to behave. It is the owner's responsibility to ensure their animal is properly trained and well-behaved to stand for hoof care, and to provide a safe environment for professionals.

Prevention & Maintenance

HOOF CARE IS ESSENTIAL FOR THE OVERALL HEALTH and well-being of horses. The hooves are a horse's foundation and are responsible for supporting the horse's weight and providing traction. A healthy foot is strong, flexible, and well-balanced, which enables a horse to move comfortably and perform at its best. On the other hand, an unhealthy hoof can cause severe pain, lameness, and even permanent damage, which can significantly affect a horse's quality of life.

Proper hoof care includes regular hoof maintenance, as well as diet and nutrition, environment and management. Regular hoof trimming and shoeing are essential for maintaining proper hoof shape and balance, which helps to redistribute weight and prevent injury. Proper diet and nutrition are also important for hoof health, as certain nutrients such as biotin, zinc, and copper are crucial for hoof growth and strength.

The environment and management of the horse also play a significant role in hoof health. A clean, dry environment is essential for preventing hoof infections, such as thrush and white line disease, and regular exercise and turnout can help to keep the hooves solid and healthy. Additionally, regular hoof care and maintenance such as cleaning and inspecting the feet can help to identify any potential problems early on and take steps to prevent them from becoming more serious.

Regular Hoof Care

Regular hoof trimming and shoeing are essential for maintaining proper hoof shape and balance, and thus it helps to redistribute weight and prevent injury. Hooves continue to grow and change over time, and regular hoof trimming is necessary to keep the feet in the correct form. Proper hoof trimming helps to redistribute weight and prevent injury.

A farrier or a veterinarian familiar with the hoof's different structures can ensure that the horse's feet are trimmed and shod in a way that promotes proper hoof balance and function. Keeping the hooves trimmed to the correct length helps to keep the horse comfortable and able to move freely.

Shoeing is also an important aspect of hoof care. Farriers can use shoes to provide extra support and protection to the hooves, especially for horses that are used for heavy work or have specific hoof conformations that require special care. Farriers can also use shoes to redistribute weight and support the affected area.

There are several factors to consider when deciding whether to trim or shoe a horse. These include:

- **The horse's use and level of activity:** The type and level of work a horse is expected to perform plays a significant role in determining whether or not to trim or shoe. For example, a horse used for heavy work or competition will require more support and protection than a horse used for light riding or pasture.

- **Hoof Conformation:** The shape and structure of a horse's hoof can also play a role in determining whether or not to trim or shoe. Horses with particular hoof conformations, such as club feet or under-run heels, may require special care and shoeing to provide additional support and redistribute weight.

- **Hoof Health:** The overall health of the horse's hooves is also an important factor to consider. A horse with healthy feet may not require shoeing, but a horse with poor hoof health may need additional support and protection to help the hooves heal.

- **Terrain and Ground surface:** The type of terrain and ground surface that the horse will be exposed to can also influence the decision to trim or shoe. For example, horses ridden on rocky or uneven terrain may require shoes to provide additional protection and support.

- **Length of time between trims:** The length of time between trim-mings is also a factor to consider when deciding to trim or shoe a horse. A horse that needs to be trimmed every 4 to 6 weeks will require more frequent shoeing than one that can go 8-10 weeks between trims.

- **Weather conditions:** Weather conditions such as rain and snow can also play a role in determining whether or not to trim or shoe a horse. Horses exposed to wet or muddy conditions may require shoes to provide additional protection and support.

Hoof Care Schedule

Following a regular hoof care schedule, horse owners can help ensure that their hooves are healthy and in good condition. This will help to pre-vent hoof problems, such as laminitis, thrush, and white line disease, and will also help to ensure that the horse is comfortable and able to move around freely. You should establish a regular hoof care schedule in consultation with a veterinarian or a farrier that considers the horse's individual needs, such as breed, age, and activity level. Here are some critical elements of a regular hoof care schedule:

- **Trimming:** Trimming is cutting or shaping the hooves to maintain proper hoof shape and function. It's essential to have the hooves trimmed regularly, typically every 4-8 weeks depending on the current rate of growth vs. rate of wear. Beyond that time, the hoof becomes long and distorted, potentially causing injury and lameness.

- **Shoeing:** Shoeing is applying metal shoes to the hooves to provide protection and support. It's essential to have the shoes checked and changed regularly, typically every 4-8 weeks. After that time, the hoof is too long and the shoes can become worn and ineffective.

- **Hoof cleaning and inspection**: Hoof cleaning and assessment should be done daily to ensure that the hooves are clean and free of debris and to identify any potential problems early on.

- **Vet check-ups**: Regular check-ups with a veterinarian can ensure the overall health of the horse's hooves. These check-ups should be scheduled based on the horse's needs and should be done at least once every six months or per the schedule suggested by veterinarian.

- **Consistency:** A regular hoof care schedule should be consistent, with regular intervals between each step, to ensure that the horse's hooves are healthy and in good condition.

Cleaning Hooves

Cleaning your horse's hooves is essential to maintaining their overall health and well-being. The hooves are the foundation of the horse, supporting its entire body and allowing them to move, run, and play. When the feet are dirty or unkempt, it can lead to various problems affecting their quality of life.

Regular hoof cleaning and inspection are essential for maintaining the health of a horse's hooves. Hoof cleaning and examination are necessary to identify potential problems early on so they can be treated before they become serious. Here are some key reasons why regular hoof cleaning and inspection are essential:

- **Detection of problems:** Regular hoof cleaning and inspection allows for the early detection of any potential issues, such as thrush, white line disease, or laminitis. You can treat these conditions more effectively if they are identified early on.

- **Preventing infection:** Hoof cleaning helps to remove dirt and debris, which can harbor bacteria and fungi that can lead to hoof infections. Regular hoof cleaning helps prevent these microorganisms' build-up and can help keep the hooves healthy.

- **Monitoring hoof growth:** Regular hoof cleaning and inspection allow for the monitoring of hoof growth. This is important for identifying potential issues, such as uneven or abnormal growth patterns, which nutritional deficiencies or other underlying conditions can cause.

- **Assessing shoeing needs:** Regular hoof cleaning and inspection allow for assessing shoeing needs. This is important for identifying any issues with the horse's current shoes, such as worn-out or ill-fitting shoes, which can cause discomfort and lead to hoof problems.

- **Checking for injuries:** Regular hoof cleaning and inspection allows for identifying any damages, such as cracks, chips, or bruises in the hoof wall, that may have occurred during turnout or exercise. Your farrier can treat these injuries more effectively if they are identified early on.

Hoof Inspection

Horse owners should regularly inspect their horse's hooves to ensure they are in good condition. Identifying the condition of a horse's feet is an integral part of hoof care, as hooves are constantly growing and changing. If any concerns are identified, a farrier or veterinarian should be consulted for further evaluation and treatment. When conducting a hoof assessment, consider the general shape and appearance of these features:

- **Shape and symmetry:** The hoof should be balanced and symmetrical, with a straight, smooth outline. The widest part of the hoof should be generally centered around the coffin joint (DIP), with approximately equal proportions front-to-back and side-to-side on a front foot. A hind foot should have the widest part slightly further to the rear of the hoof. Any deformities or distortions, such as flares, twists, dents, or lumps, indicate that a hoof is too long or out of balance. Hooves that are allowed to stay in a distorted condition for extended periods will take much longer to correct. Imbalances that begin in the limb, rather than the hoof itself, may

Balanced hoof with consistent
wear and a healthy frog

Warping

Cracks

Heel
migration

Overgrown
bars

Unhealthy frog

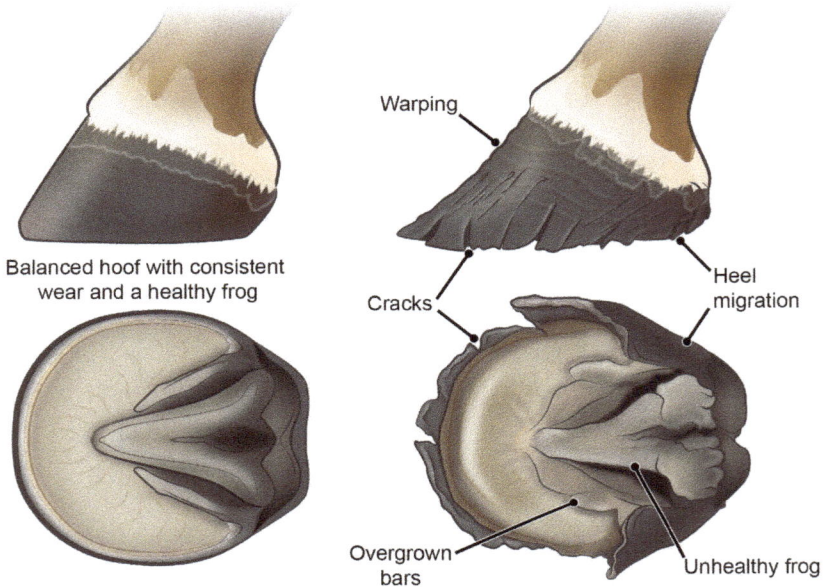

never be eliminated but can be managed with regular trimming
and shoeing for support.

- **Assess the hoof wall:** The wall of the hoof should be thick
  enough to provide adequate protection but not so thick that it
  interferes with proper function. A good rule of thumb is that the
  wall, measured from the white line to the edge of the hoof, should
  be approximately 1/4 inch thick. This thickness should be consistent all the way around the foot. If a hoof is too long, you may
  observe that the hoof wall is much thicker in the toe area while also
  stretched, thin, and brittle along the quarters. Minor chipping in
  the quarters is typical for some barefoot horses, but larger chunks
  of missing hoof wall and large cracks should be cause for concern.

- **Heel length:** The heels should be equal in height and either be
  level with or extend slightly higher than the rear-most portion of
  the frog. Heels that are too low or too high can cause pain, mis-
  aligned bones, and excessive tension on tendons and ligaments.
  The hoof wall at the heel should be straight and sturdy, not bent,

flared, curled, or crushed. Frequently, horse owners believe that their horse has "no heel" when the heels are actually under-run; the heels have length but are growing horizontally rather than vertically. Under-run horses will still need to have their heels trimmed, even though they appear too low.

- **Sole condition:** The sole of the hoof should be thick enough to provide a shock-absorbing surface for the horse's foot. You can assess sole depth by looking at the depth of the groove around the apex of the frog. A frog that sits directly on top of the sole with no indentation indicates that the soles are thin. A sole that extends above the top of the frog may be growing too thick. A too thin or too thick sole can cause sensitivity and imbalances. A healthy sole will also be free of lesions, soft spots, bruises, or other signs of trauma.

- **Frog health:** The frog of the hoof is made of the same material as the hoof wall and sole, but each of these structures has varying moisture content. The frog contains the highest moisture level and should be plump and flexible, although horses in dry environments can naturally develop a drier, harder frog. The frog should be trimmed to eliminate excessive growth and folds that harbor bacteria and reduce potential pressure points on dry, hard frogs. A healthy frog should have a wide, full appearance, while a narrow or shriveled-looking frog can indicate a hoof imbalance or disease of the frog. The central sulcus should be wide and open with a visible bottom. A deep crease in the central sulcus can cause pain and invade the sensitive frog stem, providing an opportunity for infection.

- **Signs of injury or disease:** Look for any signs of damage, such as cuts, punctures, or bruises, as well as signs of disease, such as thrush or white line disease.

- **Wear patterns:** The way a horse wears its hooves can also provide important information about their overall health and gait. Uneven wear patterns can indicate imbalances or issues with the horse's movement. An older horse, or a horse in pain, may drag its feet and cause excessive wear to the toes.

Nutrition

Proper nutrition is essential for hoof health. The hooves have many layers that are composed of different types of tissue, each with its unique nutritional requirements. Providing your horse with the right combination of protein, vitamins, and nutrients will promote strong hoof walls and healthy growth.

Forage should make up most of the horse's diet, providing important nutrients such as fiber, vitamins, and minerals. Good quality hay or grass should be fed in small amounts throughout the day to mimic a horse's natural grazing pattern.

A concentrate should be fed to provide additional energy and protein. The type and amount of concentrate will depend on the horse's needs. For example, growing horses, pregnant or lactating mares, and performance horses will have higher energy and protein requirements than sedentary adult horses.

In addition to hay and concentrate, horses may also benefit from additional supplements such as vitamins and minerals, especially if they have specific nutritional deficiencies or health conditions.

All horses have different nutritional needs depending on age, activity level, and other considerations. Monitoring the horse's body condition and weight, as well as consulting with a veterinarian or equine nutritionist about the needs of your horse, can ensure that they are getting the right balance of nutrients

Feeding recommendations for maintaining healthy hooves include:

- **Provide a balanced diet:** A well-balanced diet that provides the right balance of nutrients is essential for maintaining healthy hooves. This includes providing enough protein, vitamins, minerals, and essential fatty acids.

- **Feed high-quality hay:** Hay should be the foundation of the horse's diet. It provides a source of fiber essential for maintaining a healthy gut. High-quality hay also provides vital nutrients such as protein, vitamins, and minerals.

- **Provide a balanced source of protein:** Protein is essential for hoof growth and repair. High protein feeds such as alfalfa hay, soybean meal, or fish meal can be fed to horses with poor hoof quality.

- **Provide the right balance of minerals:** Minerals such as zinc, copper, and biotin are essential for hoof health. A balanced mineral supplement can be fed to horses that are deficient in these minerals.

- **Consider feeding a hoof supplement:** Hoof supplements contain a combination of ingredients that promote hoof health, such as biotin, zinc, methionine, lysine, and other amino acids. They can be fed to horses with poor hoof quality.

- **Limit concentrates:** Feeding too many concentrates can lead to obesity and laminitis, leading to hoof problems. Feeding too much grain or high-starch feed can also lead to an imbalance in nutrient intake, affecting hoof health.

- **Keep your horse hydrated:** Water is essential for maintaining healthy hooves. Ensuring that your horse has access to clean, fresh water is vital for maintaining overall health and hoof health.

Vitamins & Minerals

The right balance of nutrients and other essential vitamins and minerals through a well-balanced diet is vital for hoof health. Nutrients such as biotin, zinc, copper, protein, fatty acids, and vitamin A play a key role in hoof health. These nutrients help strengthen the hoof wall, promote hoof growth, maintain hoof flexibility, and improve hoof quality. Consultation with a veterinarian or nutritionist can help horse owners to provide their horses with a well-balanced diet that promotes hoof health. Some of the essential nutrients for hoof health include:

- **Biotin:** Biotin is a B vitamin that helps strengthen the hoof wall and promote growth. It is necessary to produce keratin, the protein that makes up the hoof wall, frog, and sole. A deficiency of biotin can cause weak, brittle hooves and slow hoof growth.

- **Zinc:** Zinc plays a key role in forming keratin, a significant component of the hoof wall. It is also necessary to produce collagen, which helps maintain the hooves' structural integrity. A zinc deficiency can lead to slow hoof growth, poor hoof quality, and structural abnormalities.

- **Copper:** Copper is necessary for forming collagen and elastin, which are essential components of the hoof wall and frog. Copper also plays a role in the production of melanin, which gives the hoof its color. A copper deficiency can lead to weak feet and hoof problems, as well as discoloration of the hoof.

- **Protein:** Protein is necessary for the growth and repair of the hoof. A diet that is low in protein can lead to slow hoof growth and poor hoof quality.

- **Fatty acids:** Omega-3 and Omega-6 fatty acids are essential for hoof health as they help maintain flexibility and elasticity. These fatty acids are important for the overall health of the horse.

- **Vitamin A:** Vitamin A is necessary for the growth and repair of hoof tissue. A deficiency in vitamin A can lead to dry, brittle hooves and poor hoof quality. It also plays a role in maintaining the skin's overall health, which is vital for the health of the coronary band and the hoof.

- **Vitamin C:** Vitamin C is essential for producing collagen and elastin, which are important components of the hoof wall and frog. It also plays a role in the overall health of the skin and the immune system. A deficiency in vitamin C can lead to weak hooves and hoof problems.

- **Vitamin E:** Vitamin E is an antioxidant that helps to protect the hooves from damage caused by free radicals. It also helps maintain the skin's overall health and the immune system. A deficiency in vitamin E can lead to weak hooves and hoof problems.

Body Condition Score

Horse body condition scoring is a system used to assess the amount of fat stores a horse has and to determine its overall body condition. The system assigns a numerical score to various parts of the horse's body and provides a comprehensive picture of the horse's overall weight and health. This system is used to determine whether a horse is underweight, overweight, or at an appropriate weight.

Regular monitoring of a horse's body condition score can help to prevent health problems caused by excessive weight or weight loss. An overweight horse is significantly more likely to develop laminitis, a painful and dangerous inflammation of the laminae in its hooves. It is important to remember that every horse is different, and the ideal body condition score will vary based on the horse's breed, age, and level of activity. Additionally, certain conditions such as pregnancy or illness can affect a horse's body condition score. It is best to consult with a veterinarian to determine an accurate body condition score for your horse.

The scoring process begins with the assessment of the horse's neck crest, which is located at the top of the neck. The neck crest should not be rounded, as any extra tissue in this area is fat and indicates the horse is overweight. If the neck crest is bulged or droops to one side, this indicates that the horse is obese. The next area assessed is the withers, which should have a slight hollow between them and the spine, indicating that the horse has a moderate amount of fat.

The horse's rib area is also evaluated, with the aim of being able to feel the ribs, but not see them. If the ribs are easily seen, this indicates that the horse is underweight, while if they are not easily felt, the horse is likely overweight. The horse's loin should have a slight arch, which is an indication of a moderate amount of fat.

The horse's tail head is another important area to assess, as it should have a slight fat pad, which should be visible, but not so much that it droops down. The hindquarters are also evaluated, with the aim of being able to see the hip bones, but not the spine. If the hip bones are not easily visible, this indicates that the horse is overweight.

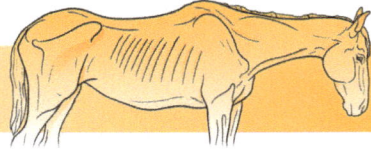

1. Poor: Extremely emaciated; no fatty tissue; vertebrae, ribs, tail head, and bones of withers, shoulder, and neck are visible.

2. Very Thin: Emaciated; slight tissue cover over bones; vertebrae, ribs, tail head, and bones of withers, shoulder, and neck are visible.

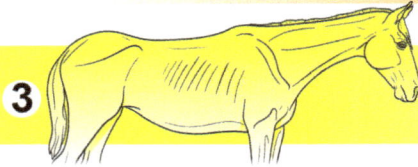

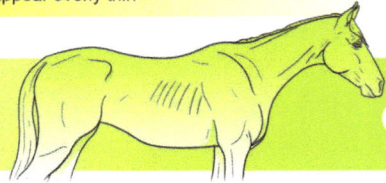

3. Thin: Slight fat cover over body; individual vertebrae and ribs no longer visibly discernible; withers, shoulders, and neck do not appear overly thin

4. Moderately Thin: Ridge of spine and outline of ribs are visible; tail head may or may not be visible depending on the breed; withers, shoulders, and neck do not appear overly thin.

5. Moderate: Spine and ribs cannot be seen however ribs can be felt; tail head is spongy; withers, shoulders, and neck are rounded and smooth.

6. Moderately Fleshy: Slight crease down spine; ribs and tail head feel spongy; fat deposits along withers and neck and behind shoulders.

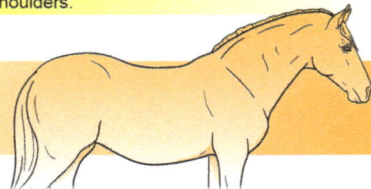

7. Fleshy: Crease down spine; ribs have fat filling between them; tail head spongy; fat deposits along withers and neck and behind shoulders.

8. Fat: Apparent crease down spine; ribs difficult to feel; soft fat surrounding tail head; fat deposits along withers, behind shoulders, and on inner thighs; neck is large.

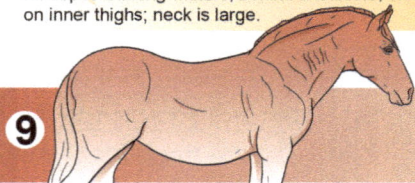

9. Extremely Fat: Obvious crease down spine; patchy fat on ribs; bulging fat on tail head, withers, behind shoulders, and on neck; fat fills in flank and on inner thighs

Horse body condition scoring (BCS) is a method used to assess the overall nutrition and fatness of a horse. The scale ranges from 1 to 9, with 1 being extremely thin and 9 being extremely overweight. The ideal body condition score for most horses is between 4 and 6. Here is a detailed explanation of each point on the horse body condition score scale:

1. **Poor:** Extremely emaciated; no fatty tissue; vertebrae, ribs, tail head, and bones of withers, shoulder, and neck are visible.

2. **Very Thin:** Emaciated; slight tissue cover over bones; vertebrae, ribs, tail head, and bones of withers, shoulder, and neck are visible.

3. **Thin:** Slight fat cover over body; individual vertebrae and ribs no longer visibly discernible; withers, shoulders, and neck do not appear overly thin.

4. **Moderately Thin:** Ridge of spine and outline of ribs are visible; tail head may or may not be visible depending on the breed; withers, shoulders, and neck do not appear overly thin.

5. **Moderate:** Spine and ribs cannot be seen however ribs can be felt; tail head is spongy; withers, shoulders, and neck are rounded and smooth.

6. **Moderately Fleshy:** Slight crease down spine; ribs and tail head feel spongy; fat deposits along withers and neck and behind shoulders.

7. **Fleshy:** Crease down spine; ribs have fat filling between them; tail head spongy; fat deposits along withers and neck and behind shoulders.

8. **Fat:** Apparent crease down spine; ribs difficult to feel; soft fat surrounding tail head; fat deposits along withers, behind shoulders, and on inner thighs; neck is large.

9. **Extremely Fat:** Obvious crease down spine; patchy fat on ribs; bulging fat on tail head, withers, behind shoulders, and on neck; fat fills in flank and on inner thighs.

Management

Throughout history, the way that horses were kept and managed has changed significantly. In the past, horses were primarily held in the wild and could roam freely, finding their own food and shelter. As human populations grew and expanded, horses were domesticated and began to be kept in stables and pastures for various purposes such as transportation, agriculture, and sports.

As our understanding of equine health and behavior has grown, so too have stall and pasture management standards. Proper management practices are crucial for maintaining horses' overall health and well-being. The horse owner's responsibility is to stay informed and ensure that their horse is kept in a safe and healthy environment.

Proper stall and pasture management include providing horses with ample space, clean bedding, and appropriate nutrition. It also involves regularly monitoring the condition of the pasture, including checking for toxic plants, mud, and uneven terrain. Additionally, it's crucial to provide horses with regular access to turnout, allowing them to move freely and graze.

Proper stall and pasture management also include sheltering horses to protect them from extreme temperatures, rain, and other weather conditions. The importance of appropriate management is reflected in the health and well-being of the horse, its overall performance, and its longevity.

Some of the critical factors include the following:

- **Flooring:** Hard, unyielding flooring, such as concrete, can be tough on hooves, leading to cracking and other hoof problems. Soft, cushioned flooring such as rubber mats or sand can help to absorb shock and reduce stress on the hooves.

- **Drainage:** Good drainage is vital to prevent moisture accumulation in the stall or pasture, which can lead to thrush and other hoof infections.

- **Lighting:** Adequate lighting allows the horse to move around safely and prevent injuries, as well as reduces stress and anxiety.

- **Turnout:** Regular turnout in a pasture is essential for hoof health as it allows the horse to move around freely and to wear down its hooves naturally. However, it's crucial to ensure the pasture is free of hazards such as rocks and holes that can cause injury.

- **Exercise:** Regular exercise is essential for hoof health as it helps to keep the hooves strong and flexible.

- **Hoof care:** Regular hoof care is vital to maintain the health of the hooves. This includes regular trimming, shoeing, and regular check-ups with a veterinarian or a farrier.

- **Cleanliness:** Keeping the stall and pasture clean and free of debris prevents the build-up of bacteria and fungi that can lead to hoof infections.

- **Climate:** The climate and weather can affect the hooves. A horse should be protected from extreme heat and cold, and the feet should be checked for signs of cracking, thrush, and other conditions caused by weather-related stress.

Clean & Dry

Maintaining a clean and dry environment for your horse is essential for their overall health and well-being and can help to ensure that their hooves stay healthy and in good condition. Here are some critical steps to take to maintain a clean and dry environment for your horse:

- **Regular cleaning:** Regularly clean the stall and pasture, removing any feces and soiled bedding. This will help to prevent the build-up of bacteria and fungus that can lead to hoof infections and other health problems.

- **Proper bedding:** Use bedding that is absorbent and easy to clean, such as wood shavings, straw, or paper. Avoid using bedding that can hold moisture, such as sawdust or sand.

- **Proper drainage:** Ensure the stall and pasture have good drainage to prevent moisture accumulation. This can be achieved by installing drainage systems, such as gutters and French drains, or by building the stall or pasture on a slight slope.

- **Adequate ventilation:** Proper ventilation is essential to maintain a healthy environment and to prevent the build-up of harmful gases such as ammonia. This can be achieved by installing windows, vents, and fans or leaving the stall door open.

- **Keep the horse clean:** Regular grooming and washing can help keep the environment clean. This includes brushing the horse's coat, cleaning its hooves, and wiping down its face and eyes.

- **Keep the feeding area clean:** Keep the feeding area clean by regularly cleaning and sanitizing the feed buckets, feeders, and water containers.

- **Keep the pasture clean:** Keep the pasture clean by regularly removing manure and other debris. This can be done using a manure fork or a manure spreader.

- **Keep the water clean:** Keep the water clean by regularly cleaning and sanitizing the water troughs, buckets, and automatic waterers.

- **Keep the environment dry:** To keep the environment dry, avoid over-watering the pasture, and use a waterproof and breathable blanket to protect the horse from wet weather.

- **Keep the environment clean:** Regularly check for hazardous materials, such as sharp objects, toxic plants, and other potential dangers.

Exercise

In our more recent history, the use of horses has shifted from transportation and agriculture towards leisure and sport. With this shift in use and decline in heavy workloads , the importance of exercise for horses has become increasingly recognized.

Horses are designed to move and graze for most of the day. In the wild, horses travel long distances, grazing on grass and foraging for food. Domestic horses, however, are often confined to small areas, such as a stall or small pastures. This lack of movement and restricted access to forage can lead to a host of health problems, including obesity, muscle, and joint problems, and behavioral issues.

Exercise is essential for maintaining a horse's physical fitness and promoting good circulation, digestion, and overall health. Exercise can also help to prevent behavioral problems and improve mental well-being. Regular exercise can improve a horse's muscle tone, increase endurance, and reduce the risk of injury.

Horses need both physical and mental stimulation to stay healthy. Turnout time in a large pasture where they can graze and move freely can provide this. Regular training, riding, and other activities provide the necessary exercise and mental stimulation.

Regular exercise and turnout are essential for hoof health. A horse's hooves are designed to withstand the constant movement and pressure of walking, running, and grazing. When a horse is confined to a stall or small paddock, they do not have the opportunity to move around and wear down their hooves naturally. This can lead to hoof problems such as overgrown hooves, contracted heels, and a lack of flexibility.

- **Exercise:** Regular exercise is vital for hoof health as it helps to keep the hooves solid and flexible. It also promotes blood flow to the feet, essential for hoof growth and repair. Exercise also helps to improve overall circulation and muscle tone, which can help to keep the horse's body in good condition.

- **Turnout:** Regular turnout in a pasture is important for hoof health as it allows the horse to move around freely and to wear down its hooves naturally. This helps to prevent hoof problems such as over-grown hooves and contracted heels. Additionally, turnout allows the horse to graze and forage, which can help to keep their diet balanced and natural.

- **Variety of terrain:** A variety of terrain is important to help promote healthy hooves. Different types of terrain, such as soft ground, hard ground, and hills, can help to wear down the feet and keep them in good condition.

- **Mental well-being:** Regular exercise and turnout are also crucial for the horse's mental well-being. Being confined to a stall or small paddock for long periods can lead to stress and behavioral problems.

By providing regular exercise and turnout, horse owners can help ensure their horse stays healthy and in good condition. Always remember that horses should be well-rested and given adequate time to rest and recover between exercise sessions. Each horse is unique, and their exercise needs will vary depending on their age, breed, and overall health. Here are a few ways that a horse owner can exercise their horse:

- **Riding:** Riding is one of the most common ways to exercise a horse. It provides a cardiovascular workout and helps to build and maintain muscle tone. Start with shorter rides and gradually increase the duration and intensity.

- **Lunging:** Lunging is a great way to exercise a horse without a rider. It involves the horse moving in circles around the handler, allowing them to work on their balance, coordination, and muscle strength. Note: precautions should be taken that lunging be performed safely and not in excess. Horses are prey animals designed to run far and fast in a straight line, not in circles. Excessive or uncontrolled lunging can lead to injury.

- **Trail Riding:** Trail riding is a great way to give your horse a change of scenery and can be an excellent workout for both horse and rider. Be aware of the trail condition and choose trails appropriate for your horse's fitness level.

- **Obstacle Course:** Building an obstacle course for your horse can be a fun way to challenge their balance, coordination, and problem-solving skills. You can use a variety of obstacles like barrels, poles, and bridges.

- **Free-jumping:** Free-jumping is a great way to help your horse develop strength, flexibility, and balance. It allows the horse to jump over several obstacles without a rider.

- **In-hand exercises:** In-hand exercises are a great way to strengthen the horse's core and improve balance and coordination. They involve leading the horse through various exercises such as lateral flexion, circles, and figure eights.

- **Round-pen work:** Round-pen work is a form of training focusing on communication and trust between horse and handler. It can be a great way to work on a horse's balance, coordination, and muscle development.

Working with Professionals

Establishing a relationship with a trusted farrier and veterinarian is critical, as communicating regularly with them ensures that the horse receives the best possible care. The farrier and the veterinarian have specialized knowledge and skills for proper care and maintenance of a horse's hooves and overall health. Here are some key reasons why it's essential to work closely with a farrier and veterinarian:

- **Expertise:** Farriers and veterinarians have specialized knowledge and expertise in the care and maintenance of horses. They can identify and treat hoof problems, such as laminitis, thrush, and white line disease, and can also identify and treat other health problems that may be related to hoof health.

- **Early detection:** By working closely with a farrier and veterinarian, horse owners can help to identify and treat potential health problems early on before they become serious. Early detection is crucial for effective treatment and minimizing the risk of complications.

■ **Monitoring of chronic conditions:** If a horse has a chronic condition such as Cushing's Disease or other metabolic disorders, regular veterinary check-ups are important for monitoring the treatment and management of these conditions.

■ **Customized care:** Working closely with a farrier and veterinarian allows for developing a customized care plan tailored to the horse's individual needs. This may include regular hoof trimming and shoeing, dietary recommendations, and exercise and turnout guidelines.

■ **Emergency care:** In case of an emergency, working closely with a farrier and veterinarian can ensure that the horse receives prompt and appropriate care.

■ **Communication:** Regular communication between the horse owner, farrier, and veterinarian is essential for ensuring that the horse's care is coordinated and that any concerns or problems are addressed promptly.

■ **Record keeping:** Working closely with a farrier and veterinarian also allows for detailed record keeping, which is important for future reference and decisions about the horse's care.

Common Hoof Problems

EARLY DETECTION AND TREATMENT OF HOOF PROBLEMS are crucial for preventing complications and ensuring the best outcome. By identifying hoof problems early on, horse owners can take steps to address the issue before it becomes more serious. Regular hoof inspections, working closely with a farrier, and regular veterinary check-ups are essential for identifying and addressing hoof problems early on. By implementing various preventative measures, horse owners can help minimize the risk of hoof problems.

Lameness

Lameness refers to an abnormal gait or limp in a horse caused by pain or discomfort in one or more limbs. Various conditions, such as injuries, infections, or degenerative diseases, can cause lameness. It can significantly impact the horse's mobility, performance, and overall well-being. Early identification of lameness is vital for preventing further damage and promoting a speedy recovery.

One of the most obvious signs of lameness in a horse is a change in its gait. A horse experiencing lameness typically has a limp or a noticeable change in its stride. They may also be reluctant to move or may be more cautious when moving around.

Another sign of lameness is pain or sensitivity when the hoof is touched or when pressure is applied to specific areas of the limb. A horse experiencing lameness may also have a decreased range of motion or may be reluctant to bear weight on the affected limb. Another indication of lameness is muscle atrophy or wasting on the affected limb, as well as increased or decreased digital pulse or heat in the limb.

In addition to these physical signs, a horse experiencing lameness may also exhibit behavioral changes. They may be more irritable or prone to biting or kicking. They may also be more inclined to stand in one spot for long periods.

To identify lameness in a horse, observe its behavior and movements closely. Pay attention to any changes in the horse's appearance, such as swelling, heat, or other signs of inflammation. If you suspect your horse may be experiencing lameness, consult with a veterinarian as soon as possible for a proper diagnosis and treatment plan.

Symptoms of lameness can include:

- Limping or favoring one limb over another
- Swelling or heat in the affected limb
- Difficulty or reluctance to move or put weight on the affected limb
- Stiffness or reluctance to bend or flex the affected limb
- Changes in the horse's stride or gait
- Shortening or lengthening of the stride
- Reduced performance or difficulty with specific movements
- Stumbling or tripping

The severity of lameness can vary widely, from mild discomfort to severe pain and disability. In some cases, the lameness may be temporary and resolved with proper care and treatment, while in other cases, it may be chronic and require ongoing management.

The diagnosis of lameness typically involves a physical examination, which may include observing the horse's gait, palpating the affected limb, and diagnostic tests such as radiography, ultrasound, and nerve blocks. In some cases, a veterinarian may need to perform a more invasive examination such as arthroscopy.

To identify lameness in horses, observe the horse's gait at a walk and a trot, as lameness may not be as evident at one gait as at another. Also, be sure to observe the horse on a hard surface and a soft surface, as the horse may be more or less lame on a different footing.

When observing the horse's gait, look for signs of asymmetry, such as a shorter stride on one limb, a limb being held off the ground longer than usual, or a limb being placed on the ground with less force. Observing the horse's body posture is also important, as a horse may shift weight to compensate for lameness in one limb.

To observe abnormalities in a horse's gait, watch the horse walk and trot in a straight line and a circle in both directions , as this will allow you to see the horse's movement from different angles. Pay attention to the horse's leg movement, looking for any asymmetry or unevenness in the horse's stride.

A normal gait for a horse is smooth, balanced, and symmetrical. A horse moving with a normal gait will have a smooth and rhythmic movement, with each footfall following a consistent pattern. Four basic gaits are considered normal for a horse: walk, trot, canter, and gallop.

- At the walk, the horse should take four beats, and usually follow this sequence: left hind leg, left front leg, right hind leg, right front leg. At the walk, the horse will alternate between having three or two feet on the ground. The horse should have a smooth and relaxed movement, with the head and tail held in a natural position.

- At the trot, the horse should take two beats, with diagonal pairs of legs moving together, meaning that the front leg is paired with the opposite hind.The horse should have a balanced and symmetrical movement, with the head and tail held in a natural position.

- The canter is a three beat gait where one pair of feet strike the ground simultaneously and the other two feet land independently. The canter will either be on what is called a "right lead" or "left lead". On the "right lead", the hoof pattern is left hind, right hind and left front simultaneously, then right front - the right front will stretch out furthest, hence "right lead". "Left lead" as follows: right hind, left hind and right front simultaneously, left front.

- At a gallop, the gait will be similar to a canter and have left and right leads, however the gait will be faster and will have four distinct beats. There will be a moment of suspension where all four feet are off the ground at once. The horse should have a smooth and powerful movement, with the head and tail held in a natural position.

Pay attention to the horse's behavior, such as reluctance to move, reluctance to bear weight on a limb, or shifting weight frequently. It is also essential to pay attention to the horse's body posture and movement, as any asymmetry or unevenness in the horse's body movement can indicate an underlying problem. In addition to observing the horse's movement, the horse owner should also pay attention to the horse's body language and overall demeanor. A horse in pain or discomfort will have a different body language and behavior than a horse that is moving normally.

Several grading scales are commonly used to describe the severity of lameness in horses. One of the most widely used scales is the American Association of Equine Practitioners (AAEP) lameness grading scale, which ranges from 0 to 5.

The AAEP lameness grading scale is as follows:

- **Grade 0:** Lameness not perceptible under any circumstances.

- **Grade 1:** Lameness is difficult to observe and is not consistently apparent, regardless of circumstances (e.g. under saddle, circling, inclines, hard surface, etc.).

- **Grade 2:** Lameness is difficult to observe at a walk or when trotting in a straight line but consistently apparent under certain circumstances (e.g. weight-carrying, circling, inclines, hard surface, etc.).

- **Grade 3:** Lameness is consistently observable at a trot under all circumstances.

- **Grade 4:** Lameness is obvious at a walk.

- **Grade 5:** Lameness produces minimal weight bearing in motion and/or at rest or a complete inability to move.

It's important to note that while these scales can provide a general idea of the severity of lameness, they are not always precise and should be used in conjunction with a veterinarian's examination and other diagnostic tools to make an accurate diagnosis.

After discovering a horse is experiencing a lameness issue, multiple methods of testing may be employed to locate the effected area and underlying cause of lameness. Some of these tests may be performed by the horse owner and the information relayed to the professional can be very helpful, while other testing may need to be performed by a farrier or veterinarian.

- **Visual examination:** This examination will look for any obviously visible signs of injury. Open wounds, blood, discharge, or swelling can be an immediate indication that something is wrong.

- **Palpation:** This refers to feeling the horse's legs and body to locate areas that may be painful to the touch or to identify locations of swelling that are not obvious to the eyes. This includes the use of hoof testers, which are a specialized tool used by farriers and vets, to pinpoint areas of pain or sensitivity in the hoof capsule.

- **Vital signs:** Checking a horse's temperature, respiratory rate, and pulse can offer insight into possible diseases or infections causing lameness issues. Specifically, high heat and a strong pulse near the hoof may point to laminitis or an infection in the hoof.

- **Flexion test:** Can be used to identify lameness originating in a joint or soft tissue. Manual pressure is applied to flex an entire limb, or a specific joint, and the horse is asked to walk or trot to see if the manipulation has had any effect to increase or decrease the lameness.

- **Veterinary diagnostics:** When other options have failed to identify the source of lameness, a veterinarian may resort to advanced diagnostic techniques, including: x-rays, ultrasound imaging, MRIs, CT scans, or blood tests.

Treatment for lameness will depend on the underlying cause and may include the following:

- **Rest and confinement:** Rest is an essential treatment for lameness. The horse should be kept in a stall or small pen and provided with soft, deep bedding to minimize stress on the affected limb.

- **Pain management:** Pain medication will be administered to alleviate pain and discomfort.

- **Cold therapy:** Cold therapy can reduce inflammation and swelling in the affected area.

- **Supportive shoeing:** The horse may be fitted with a therapeutic shoe or pad to provide additional support and protection to the affected hoof.

- **Physical therapy:** Physical therapy may help the horse regain strength and range of motion in the affected limb.

- **Surgery:** In some cases, surgery may be necessary to repair the damage.

It is important to follow the veterinarian's instructions and provide proper care and management during recovery to ensure the best outcome. Regular follow-up appointments with the veterinarian will be needed to monitor the healing progress and make necessary adjustments to the treatment plan.

Laminitis

Laminitis is a serious and painful condition affecting the sensitive structures within the horse's hooves. It is caused by inflammation in the laminae, the interlocking layers of tissue that connect the horse's coffin bone to the hoof wall. When these tissues become inflamed, they can become damaged, leading to various problems in the horse's hooves.

The exact cause of laminitis is not fully understood, but it is believed to be related to a number of factors. Some of the most common causes of laminitis include obesity, diet, high insulin, hormonal imbalances and decreased blood flow. In obese horses, the added weight on the hooves can cause increased stress on the laminae, leading to inflammation and laminitis. A diet high in non-structural carbohydrates (NSCs), such as sugars and starches, can also contribute to laminitis. Hormonal imbalances such as Cushing's disease and insulin resistance can also lead to laminitis, as they can cause changes in the horse's metabolism that affect the hooves.

Mild/ Acute

P2

P3   N

Inflammation

Moderate

P2

N

P3

Lamellar
tearing

P3 sinking

Severe/ Chronic

Distorted
hoof wall

P2

N

P3

Tissue
damage

Lamellar
wedge

P3 rotation and
degradation

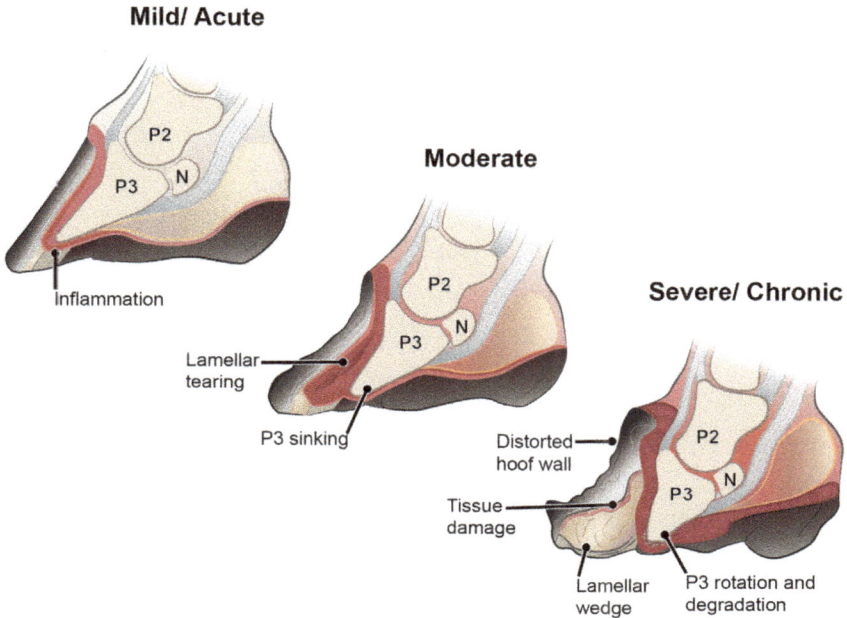

Obesity is one of the most common causes of laminitis in horses. When a horse is overweight, it puts additional stress on the hooves, which can cause inflammation in the laminae and lead to laminitis. The added weight on the feet can cause increased pressure on the sensitive structures within the hoof, leading to inflammation and damage. Obesity can also cause changes in the horse's metabolism that affect the hooves, making the horse more susceptible to laminitis.

Diet is also a significant factor in the development of laminitis. A diet high in non-structural carbohydrates (NSCs), such as sugars and starches, can contribute to laminitis. Bacteria easily ferment NSCs in the hindgut, which can cause an increase in acidity and a decrease in pH. This can lead to inflammation in the laminae and the development of laminitis. Additionally, high levels of NSCs can cause changes in the horse's metabolism that affect the hooves, making the horse more susceptible to laminitis.

Hormonal imbalances such as Cushing's disease and insulin resistance can also lead to laminitis. Cushing's disease is a condition that affects the pituitary gland and causes it to produce too much of the hormone ACTH, which can lead to changes in the horse's metabolism that affect the hooves. Insulin resistance is a condition in which the horse's body becomes less responsive to the hormone insulin, which can cause changes in the horse's metabolism that affect the hooves. Both of these conditions can make a horse more susceptible to laminitis.

Trauma, as well as certain medical conditions such as sepsis, can also cause laminitis. The inflammation caused by these conditions can affect the laminae and lead to laminitis. Additionally, some drugs and certain medical treatments can lead to laminitis as a side effect.

Symptoms

Laminitis is a serious condition that can cause a variety of symptoms in horses. Some of the most common signs of laminitis include lameness, heat, and pain in the hooves.

Lameness is one of the first signs of laminitis and is often the most noticeable symptom. The horse may appear uncomfortable when standing and shift its weight frequently or stand with its front legs stretched out in front and its hind legs tucked under. The horse may also have a shortened stride or be unwilling to move or bear weight on the affected limb. This can signify that the horse is experiencing pain in the hooves.

Heat and pain in the hooves are also common symptoms of laminitis. The horse's hooves may become warm to the touch and the horse may have a digital pulse, which is a sign of inflammation. Pain may be present when the hoof is palpated, especially in the toe/sole area, and the horse may be reluctant to move or bear weight on the affected limb. The inflammation of the laminae within the hoof can cause these symptoms.

As the condition progresses, the hooves may become sensitive to the touch and the horse may be reluctant to have them handled. The horse may also appear to be in pain when standing and may be unwilling to move. The horse may also develop a "founder stance" characterized by a tucked-up abdominal position, and an elevated front end, with the hind end being lower. This is a sign that the horse's hooves cannot support the horse's weight properly, and the horse is trying to take pressure off the front feet.

Progression of laminitis can lead to a more severe condition called founder. Founder occurs when the horse's hooves can no longer support the weight of the horse. This is caused by the separation of the coffin bone from the hoof wall, which can lead to the rotation and/or sinking of the bone. As the bone rotates and sinks, it can cause severe pain and the horse may be unable to stand or move. Founder is a painful and often irreversible condition that can cause long-term damage to the horse's hooves and can affect the horse's overall health and well-being.

Diagnosis

Laminitis is a complex condition assessed through a variety of diagnostic tools. Diagnosis of laminitis typically involves a physical examination and x-rays of the hooves. A veterinarian will thoroughly examine the horse, looking for signs of lameness, heat, and pain in the hooves. They will also take the horse's temperature, pulse, and respiration and check for inflammation.

X-rays are the most helpful diagnostic tool for laminitis. They allow the veterinarian to see the inside of the hoof and to check the position and shape of the coffin bone, which can be affected by laminitis. X-rays can also check for other conditions that cause lameness, such as fractures or infections.

The veterinarian may also perform blood tests to check for hormonal imbalances that may contribute to the development of laminitis. These tests can check for conditions such as Cushing's disease and insulin resistance, which can cause changes in the horse's metabolism that affect the hooves.

Treatment

Treatment for laminitis can vary depending on the severity of the condition, but generally requires a multi-faceted treatment approach that involves reducing inflammation and providing support to the affected hooves. This may include medications to reduce pain and inflammation and hoof support such as special shoes or pads. Managing diet and weight is also essential, as well as providing a dry and comfortable environment for the horse. Surgery may sometimes be required to remove damaged tissue or realign the hooves. A DDFT tenotomy reduces the strain on the coffin bone and can help to alleviate severe rotation of the bone.

Pain management is an essential aspect of treatment for laminitis. Analgesics such as non-steroidal anti-inflammatory drugs (NSAIDs) may be used to reduce inflammation and manage pain. Other pain management options, such as nerve blocks or epidurals, may provide additional pain relief in more severe cases.

Hoof support is another crucial aspect of treatment for laminitis. This can include specialized shoeing or hoof pads, which can help redistribute the horse's weight and take pressure off the affected hooves. In some cases, a veterinarian may recommend using a cast or other type of support to help stabilize the hooves and promote healing.

Dietary changes are also an essential aspect of treatment for laminitis. A diet low in non-structural carbohydrates (NSCs) such as sugars and starches is recommended for horses with laminitis. This can help to reduce the risk of acidosis and inflammation in the laminae. Additionally, providing the horse with a balanced diet that includes a variety of vitamins and minerals can help to promote hoof health.

Surgery may be necessary in more severe cases to correct the bone position and help the horse recover.

Prevention

Maintaining a healthy diet and weight, providing a dry and comfortable environment, and regular hoof care and veterinary check-ups can all aid in the prevention of laminitis. While we can significantly minimize the risk of laminitis, this condition is not entirely preventable because of onsets due to illness or mechanical strain.

Prevention is critical when managing laminitis and maintaining the overall health of your horse's hooves. Here are some essential prevention methods to keep in mind:

- **Proper diet and exercise:** Maintaining a healthy weight and body condition score is vital to prevent laminitis. Feeding a diet low in non-structural carbohydrates (NSCs) such as sugars and starches can help to reduce the risk of acidosis and inflammation in the laminae. Additionally, providing the horse with a balanced diet that includes a variety of vitamins and minerals can help to promote hoof health. Use caution when allowing horses to graze, as they can quickly overeat fresh spring grass. Regular exercise can also help control the horse's weight and maintain overall health.

- **Regular veterinary check-ups:** Regular check-ups with a veterinarian are important to detect any signs of hoof problems early on. The veterinarian will check the horse's pulse and temperature and check for inflammation. The vet may also perform hoof X-rays to check for any signs of laminitis.

- **Regular farrier care:** A regular hoof trimming and shoeing schedule can help maintain proper hoof shape and function.

- **Monitoring the horse's weight and body condition score:** Obesity is one of the main risk factors for laminitis, so tracking the horse's weight and body condition score is vital to prevent it.

Laminitis is a serious condition that can be prevented by maintaining a healthy diet and exercise and paying attention to changes in your horse's appearance and behavior. It is vital to take an active role in your horse's hoof care and to work closely with a veterinarian and farrier to identify and address any potential hoof problems early on.

Hoof Abscesses

A hoof abscess is a pocket of infection that develops within the horse's hoof. They can occur in any part of the hoof but are most common in the heel area. Hoof abscesses are caused by bacterial or fungal infections that enter the hoof through a break in the hoof wall, a crack in the sole, or a puncture wound. Damage to the hoof can also cause abscesses.

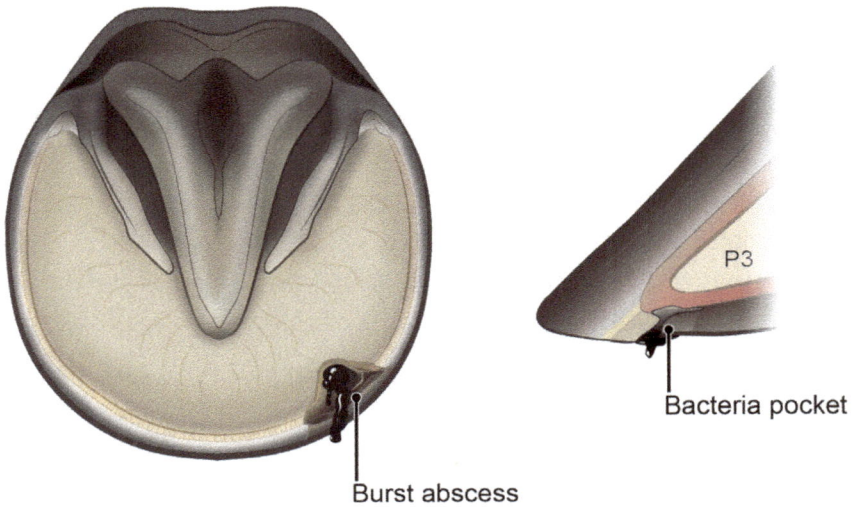

Bacteria pocket

Burst abscess

- **Trauma:** Trauma to the hoof is one of the most common causes of hoof abscesses. A puncture wound, bruise, or crack in the hoof can allow bacteria or fungus to enter the foot and cause an infection.

- **Poor Hoof Hygiene:** Poor hoof hygiene can also contribute to the development of abscesses. If the hoof is not kept clean and dry, bacteria and fungus can thrive, leading to infection.

- **Pedal Osteitis:** Pedal osteitis is a condition in which the bone within the hoof becomes inflamed. This can occur due to injury, infection, or poor blood supply to the bone. Pedal osteitis can lead to the formation of an abscess.

- **Genetics:** Some horses may be predisposed to hoof abscesses due to genetic factors.

- **Environmental factors:** Exposure to wet and dirty environments can increase the risk of a hoof abscess.

- **Nutrition:** Nutritional deficiencies can lead to poor hoof health, making the horse more susceptible to hoof abscesses.

It is important to note that hoof abscesses can also be a complication of another underlying hoof condition, such as laminitis, navicular syndrome, or white line disease. Therefore, early detection and prompt treatment are vital in preventing hoof abscesses and their underlying causes.

Symptoms

Hoof abscesses can cause various symptoms, the most common of which is lameness. Not all horses will display the same symptoms, and some horses may be less vocal about their pain. The most common symptoms of abscesses may include:

- **Lameness:** The horse may be lame in the affected hoof, and the lameness may be severe. As the abscess progresses, the lameness may become more pronounced.

- **Heat:** The affected area may be warm to the touch, indicating inflammation and infection.

- **Swelling:** There may be swelling in the affected area, particularly in the heel or sole of the hoof.

- **Discharge:** As the abscess matures, it may rupture and release pus, which is usually foul-smelling.

- **Sensitivity:** The horse may be sensitive to hoof testers in the affected area, flinching or pulling away when touching the site.

- **General unwellness:** Some horses may appear unwell, with a loss of appetite and fever.

Diagnosis

Diagnosis of a hoof abscess typically involves a visual examination of the hoof and hoof testers to identify the specific area of pain. In some cases, your vet may also use x-rays to determine the extent of the abscess and check for any underlying structural issues. No single test can diagnose a hoof abscess, and the veterinarian or farrier may use a combination of these methods:

- **Visual examination:** Your farrier or veterinarian will visually inspect the hoof, looking for signs of swelling, heat, or discharge. They may also use hoof testers to identify the specific area of pain.

- **Radiographs:** Radiographs (x-rays) can be used to confirm the presence of an abscess, determine the extent of the abscess and check for any underlying structural issues.

- **Digital Palpation:** Digital palpation, which is the use of fingers to examine the affected area, can locate the abscess and detect any pain or swelling.

- **Nuclear Scintigraphy:** Nuclear scintigraphy is a diagnostic imaging test that uses a small amount of radioactive material and a specialized camera to create detailed images of the bone structures in the hoof. It can be used to detect an abscess that is located deep in the foot.

- **Ultrasound:** Ultrasound can be used to detect an abscess and determine the size and location of the abscess.

- **Blood test:** Blood tests can be helpful to detect signs of infection in the body that may be related to the hoof abscess.

Treatment

Treatment methods will vary depending on the severity of the abscess and the underlying cause, but typically involves relieving pain, reducing inflammation, and eliminating the infection. Removing dirt and debris from the hoof and creating an opening for the abscess to drain can be beneficial, as well as the use of antibiotics or antifungal medications to combat the infection. Several methods can be used to treat a hoof abscess, including:

- **Poultice:** A poultice can be applied to the affected area to draw out the infection and reduce inflammation. A poultice is a warm, moist compress that can be made from materials such as clay, Epsom salt, or sugar.

- **Soaking:** Soaking the affected hoof in warm water can help to soften the abscess and encourage it to rupture.

- **Medications:** While medication may occasionally be prescribed in extreme cases, antibiotics and anti-inflammatory drugs are often not helpful and may even hinder the healing of an abscess. Although abscesses are bacterial infections, the most routinely available antibiotics for horses do not generally reach the hoof in concentrations enough to be helpful and do not target the bacteria which commonly cause abscesses. Additionally, medications can slow the maturation of the abscess and prolong the course of the disease.

- **Hoof support:** A shoe or pad may be applied to the affected hoof to provide support and protect the abscess as it heals.

- **Surgery:** In cases where the abscess is deep in the hoof and not responsive to other treatment methods, surgery may be needed to drain the abscess and remove any infected tissue.

- **Rest:** Rest is an integral part of treatment, as the horse needs time to recover and allow the abscess to heal. In some cases, hand walking may be encouraged to expedite drainage of the abscess.

- **Follow-up care:** Regular follow-up care is vital to ensure that the abscess has fully healed and to detect any recurrence.

Prevention

To prevent a hoof abscess, it's essential to practice good hoof hygiene. Here are several methods that can be used to avoid hoof abscesses:

- **Regular hoof care:** Regular hoof care, including regular trimming and shoeing, can help to prevent abscesses by keeping the hooves in good condition and identifying any issues early on.

- **Proper hygiene:** Keeping the hooves clean and dry can help to avoid abscesses by reducing the risk of infection.

- **Proper nutrition:** A well-balanced diet that includes adequate amounts of protein, vitamins, and minerals can help to promote strong and healthy hooves, reducing the risk of abscesses.

- **Proper exercise:** Regular exercise can help to maintain strong hooves and reduce the risk of abscesses caused by poor conformation or overuse.

- **Regular veterinary check-ups:** Regular veterinary check-ups can help to identify any underlying conditions that may increase the risk of abscesses, such as pedal osteitis or laminitis.

- **Proper shoeing and trimming:** Proper shoeing and trimming can help keep the hooves balanced and reduce the risk of abscesses caused by improper weight-bearing.

- **Good stall and pasture management:** Proper stall and pasture management can help to reduce the risk of abscesses by providing a clean and dry environment for your horse.

Thrush

Thrush is a bacterial infection that affects the horse's hooves, specifically the frog and the central sulcus of the frog. Thrush can cause pain and discomfort for the horse and lead to more severe hoof problems if left untreated. The bacteria can damage the sensitive tissues of the hoof, making it more susceptible to other infections or injuries. It can also cause structural damage to the foot, leading to lameness or other problems.

Thrush is caused by the overgrowth of anaerobic bacteria in the horse's hooves. These bacteria thrive in warm and moist environments, such as dirty or wet stall floors or pastures, and can infect the horse's hooves through minor cuts or puncture wounds.

Some of the most common causes of thrush include:

- **Poor hygiene:** Dirty or wet conditions in the horse's stall or pasture can create an ideal environment for the growth of bacteria. Horse hooves are in contact with the ground and are exposed to dirt, feces, and urine, making a perfect breeding ground for bacteria if not cleaned regularly.

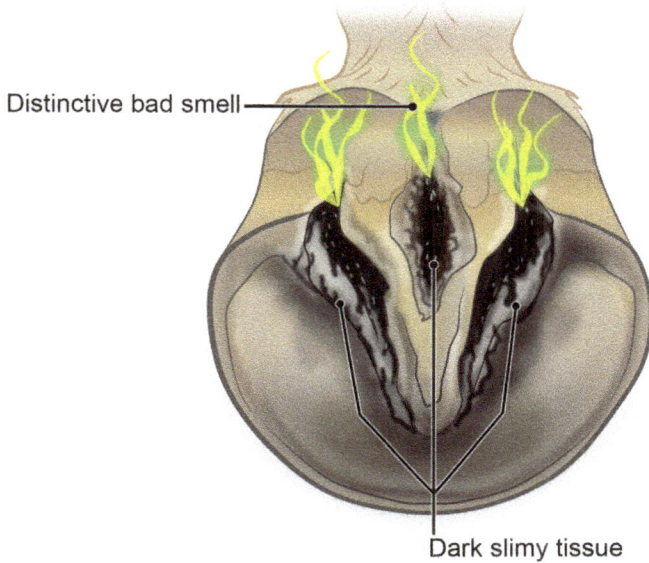

Distinctive bad smell

Dark slimy tissue

- **Wet conditions:** Wet conditions can soften the hoof, making it more susceptible to infection. This can occur in areas with high precipitation or in horses that are kept in flooded or muddy pastures.

- **Trauma to the hoof:** Trauma to the hoof, such as a puncture wound or a bruise, can create an opening for bacteria to enter the foot.

- **Overuse of antibiotics:** Overuse of antibiotics can lead to the development of antibiotic-resistant strains of bacteria, making it more challenging to treat thrush.

- **Immune-compromised horses:** Horses with weakened immune systems are more susceptible to bacterial infections, including thrush.

- **Unbalanced diet:** A diet that lacks essential vitamins and minerals can lead to poor hoof health, making it more susceptible to thrush.

Symptoms

Not all horses will show visible symptoms of thrush, but if the condition is left untreated, it can cause pain and discomfort for the horse. It can also lead to more severe hoof problems, such as structural damage to the hoof, which can lead to lameness or other issues. It's important to check the hooves regularly, and if you suspect thrush, seek veterinary care as soon as possible to prevent it from progressing and causing more severe issues.

The symptoms of thrush can include:

- **Foul odor:** One of the most notable symptoms of thrush is a strong, foul odor coming from the horse's hooves. This is caused by the bacteria producing gases as they break down the tissues in the hoof.

- **Black discharge:** Another common symptom of thrush is black discharge from the affected area. This discharge is a mixture of bacteria, dead tissue, and other debris.

- **Lameness:** The horse may appear to be uncomfortable or lame and may have difficulty standing or moving.

- **Sensitivity:** The horse may be sensitive to touch or pressure on the affected hoof, especially on the frog and central sulcus.

- **Swelling:** The affected area may be swollen, and the frog may be flattened or sunken.

- **Cracks and white line separation:** The thrush can cause separation of the white line, which is the line between the hoof wall and the sole. The hoof wall may also develop cracks.

Diagnosis

Diagnosis of thrush typically involves a visual examination of the horse's hooves and a physical examination.

- **Visual examination:** The veterinarian will look for signs of thrush, such as a strong, foul odor coming from the horse's hooves, as well as black discharge from the affected area. The veterinarian may also observe the horse's gait and check for any signs of lameness or discomfort.

- **Hoof testers:** Hoof testers, which are specialized pliers, are used to apply pressure to different parts of the hoof. They are used to identify areas of pain or sensitivity, which can help pinpoint affected areas.

- **Digital pulse:** The veterinarian may also use a digital pulse to check for inflammation and gauge the thrush's severity.

- **Cultures:** In some cases, the veterinarian may take a culture of the discharge to identify the specific type of bacteria causing the thrush. This can guide treatment options.

- **Radiographs:** In advanced cases, radiographs may be taken to evaluate any damage to the hoof structures.

While thrush can be diagnosed visually, having a veterinarian or a farrier confirm the diagnosis and rule out other conditions that may cause similar symptoms is important. Once the diagnosis of thrush is established, the veterinarian will determine the best course of treatment for the horse based on the severity of the infection, the underlying cause, and any other factors contributing to the horse's condition.

Treatment

Treatment for thrush typically involves a combination of cleaning the affected area and the use of antifungal and antibacterial medications.

- **Cleaning the affected area:** The first step in treating thrush is to clean the affected area. This involves removing debris and bacteria from the hoof using a hoof pick and a stiff brush. The site should be cleaned thoroughly to remove as much bacteria as possible.

- **Topical Medications:** The affected area can be treated with topical medications such as iodine, chlorhexidine, or copper sulfate. These medications work by killing the bacteria and preventing further growth.

- **Systemic Medications:** In some cases, the veterinarian may prescribe oral antibiotics or antifungal medications. These medications work by killing the bacteria and preventing further growth.

- **Hoof packing:** The affected area can also be packed with a medicated hoof pack or poultice to help draw out the infection and promote healing.

- **Trimming and Shoeing:** The farrier may also need to trim and shoe the horse's hooves to remove any infected or damaged tissue and to improve the horse's footing.

Even effective treatment for thrush can take several weeks or months, depending on the severity of the infection. The horse's hooves will need to be closely monitored to ensure that the infection is cleared and that the horse is comfortable.

Prevention

Preventing thrush involves maintaining a clean and dry environment for your horse and providing proper care for their hooves. It requires consistent effort, and regular maintenance is crucial to keep the horse's hooves healthy and clean.

- **Proper cleaning and maintenance of the hooves:** One of the most effective ways to prevent thrush is to maintain a clean and dry environment for your horse. This includes regular cleaning of the horse's hooves, removing debris, and ensuring that the horse is kept in a clean and dry stall or pasture.

- **Proper hygiene:** Keeping the hooves clean by picking them out daily, trimming the frog, and keeping the area clean can also help prevent thrush. This can be done by regularly cleaning the hooves with a stiff brush and using a hoof pick to remove any debris.

- **Proper diet and exercise:** Proper diet and regular exercise can help maintain overall hoof health, including preventing thrush. A balanced diet that includes the necessary vitamins and minerals for hoof health and regular exercise can help to promote strong, healthy hooves.

- **Regular veterinary check-ups:** Regular veterinary check-ups can help identify and address any potential hoof problems early on, including thrush, before progressing to more severe issues.

- **Proper shoeing and trimming:** Regular shoeing and trimming can help to promote good hoof health and to prevent conditions such as thrush. A farrier can help ensure that the horse's hooves are trimmed and shod correctly to support the horse's weight and keep the hoof neatly trimmed to prevent thrush.

White Line Disease

White line disease is a condition that affects the white line (laminae), which is the line between the hoof wall and the sole of the horse's hoof. The disease is caused by a fungal infection that invades the white line and causes it to weaken and separate. It is a progressive condition that, if left untreated, can lead to severe structural damage to the hoof.

Several factors, including poor hoof hygiene, exposure to moisture, and other underlying conditions, can cause the infection.

- **Poor hoof hygiene:** One of the most common causes of white line disease is poor hoof hygiene. This can include neglecting to clean the hooves regularly, not removing debris, or not providing proper care for the horse's hooves.

- **Exposure to moisture:** White line disease can also be caused by moisture, such as standing in wet or muddy conditions. Moisture can soften the hoof and make it more susceptible to fungal infections.

- **Nutritional deficiencies:** Nutritional deficiencies can also make the horse susceptible to white line disease. A lack of essential vitamins and minerals, particularly biotin and zinc, can cause the hooves to become weak and brittle, making them more susceptible to fungal infections.

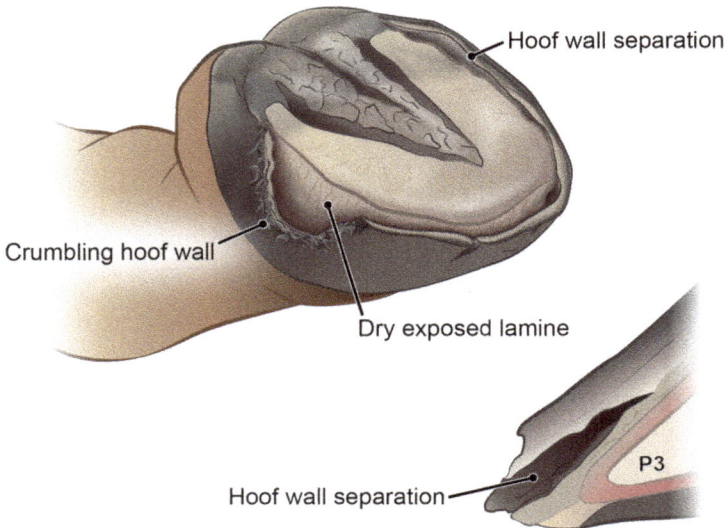

- **Hormonal imbalances:** Hormonal imbalances, such as Cushing's disease or Equine Metabolic Syndrome, can also lead to the development of white line disease.

- **Trauma:** Trauma to the hoof can also cause white line disease. This can include injuries such as punctures, cuts, bruises, or other types of trauma such as overreaching or interference.

- **Genetics:** Some horses may be genetically predisposed to white line disease, making them more susceptible to the condition.

Symptoms

The symptoms of white line disease may not appear all at once and may take some time to develop. Additionally, the symptoms may vary depending on the severity of the infection and the stage of the disease. Generally, the condition can cause several symptoms, including:

- **Lameness:** One of the most common symptoms of white line disease is lameness. The horse may appear to be uncomfortable or lame and may have difficulty standing or moving.

- **Separation of the white line:** The white line may appear to be widened or separated, and the hoof wall may pull away from the sole. The veterinarian or the farrier can observe this.

- **Crumbling of the hoof wall:** The affected area may appear to be crumbly or flaky. This can be caused by the fungal infection breaking down the structural integrity of the hoof.

- **Smelly discharge:** The affected area may be producing a foul-smelling discharge. This is caused by the fungal infection breaking down the dead tissue and releasing the gases that cause the smell.

- **Sensitivity:** The horse may be sensitive to touch or pressure on the affected area of the hoof. The horse may flinch or pull away when the foot is touched or picked up.

- **Reduced hoof growth:** The affected hoof may grow more slowly than the others. The farrier or the veterinarian can observe this during regular check-ups

Diagnosis

A veterinarian or a farrier can determine infection of white line disease through a visual examination of the hooves. The following methods are commonly used to diagnose the condition:

- **Visual examination:** The veterinarian or farrier will examine the hooves for signs of white line disease, such as separation of the white line, crumbling of the hoof wall, and foul-smelling discharge. They may also check for other signs of lameness, such as heat and pain in the hooves.

- **Hoof testers:** Hoof testers are specialized tools that allow the veterinarian or farrier to apply pressure to different parts of the hoof to identify any areas of pain or sensitivity. This can help confirm the white line disease diagnosis, as the affected area will typically be more sensitive to pressure than the rest of the hoof.

- **X-rays:** In some cases, the veterinarian may also take x-rays of the hoof to determine the extent of the infection and structural damage. X-rays can provide a clear image of the bones and the internal structures of the hoof, which can help to confirm the diagnosis.

- **Laboratory tests:** In some cases, the veterinarian may take a sample of the discharge or the tissue of the affected area and send it to a laboratory for analysis. This can help identify the specific type of fungus causing the infection.

Treatment

Treatment for white line disease can be time-consuming and may require multiple visits to the farrier or veterinarian. The treatment may need to be adjusted based on the horse's response and the infection's severity, and the horse may need to be on stall rest for some time to allow the hoof to heal and recover. Treatment for white line disease typically involves a combination of methods to clean the affected area, remove the fungal infection, and prevent it from recurring. The following are some of the most common treatment options:

- **Cleaning the affected area:** The first step in treating white line disease is to clean the affected area. This can involve removing any debris, such as dirt and manure, from the hoof and removing any loose or crumbly hoof wall. The affected area should be cleaned thoroughly with a hoof pick or a stiff brush.

- **Medications:** Antifungal and antibacterial medications may be used to treat the infection. These medications can be applied topically to the affected area or may be given orally. Some common remedies include:

- Topical treatments such as iodine, chlorhexidine, or copper sulfate

- Oral antifungal medications such as itraconazole, terbinafine, and griseofulvin

- **Hoof support:** Hoof support is integral to treating white line disease. This can consist of special shoes or pads that can help to redistribute the horse's weight and take pressure off the affected area. Additionally, the farrier may use a special adhesive to help keep the hoof wall in place and prevent further separation.

■ **Diet and management:** Diet and management are also essential to treating white line disease. Horse owners should provide a balanced diet that includes all essential vitamins and minerals, especially biotin and zinc, to support hoof health. Also, proper hygiene and management practices, such as providing a dry environment and regular hoof cleaning, can help prevent the condition from recurring.

Prevention

Prevention is vital to avoiding hoof problems such as white line disease. The prevention of white line disease is ongoing, and horse owners should maintain proper hoof hygiene and management practices throughout the horse's life.

The following are some of the most effective methods for preventing the condition:

■ **Proper hoof hygiene:** Regular cleaning and inspection of the hooves are essential to prevent the buildup of debris, such as dirt and manure, that can provide an environment for the fungus to thrive. Weekly cleaning of the hoofs with a hoof pick, stiff brush, and cleaning solution is recommended.

■ **Providing a dry environment:** White line disease thrives in damp environments. Horse owners should provide their horses with a clean, dry environment, including a well-drained stall and pasture. Additionally, the use of moisture-wicking bedding can help to keep the hooves dry.

■ **Regular farrier check-ups:** A regular farrier check-up schedule is crucial for preventing hoof problems. The farrier can identify and address any issues before they become serious. Additionally, regular trimming and shoeing can help maintain proper hoof shape and balance, preventing the development of white line disease.

- **Proper diet and management:** Proper diet and management are also crucial for avoiding hoof problems. A balanced diet that includes all essential vitamins and minerals, especially biotin and zinc, is vital for hoof health. Also, proper management practices, such as regular exercise and turnout, can help maintain healthy hooves.

- **Early detection:** Early detection is crucial for preventing white line disease from progressing and causing more severe damage to the foot. Horse owners should be aware of the symptoms of white line disease and should seek veterinary or farrier attention if they notice any signs of the condition.

Navicular Syndrome

Navicular syndrome is a condition that affects the navicular bone and the surrounding structures in the horse's hoof. It is characterized by inflammation and degeneration of the navicular bone and the supporting structures, such as the deep digital flexor tendon and the ligaments that attach the navicular bone to the coffin bone. This can cause pain and lameness in the horse, especially when the horse is asked to move on hard surfaces or to make tight turns.

The exact cause of navicular syndrome is not well understood and can be challenging to diagnose and treat, as it presents similarly to other hoof conditions. Navicular syndrome is thought to be caused by a combination of factors; the following are some of the most commonly cited causes:

- **Conformation:** Horses with specific conformations, such as a high-crested neck and a short back, are more prone to developing navicular syndrome. This is because these conformations can place added stress on the navicular bone and the surrounding structures.

- **Genetics:** Some studies have suggested that there may be a genetic component to the development of navicular syndrome. Horses with a family history of the condition may be more likely to develop it themselves.

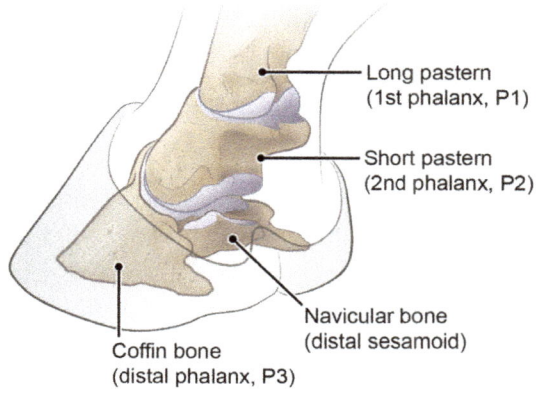

Long pastern
(1st phalanx, P1)

Short pastern
(2nd phalanx, P2)

Navicular bone
(distal sesamoid)

Coffin bone
(distal phalanx, P3)

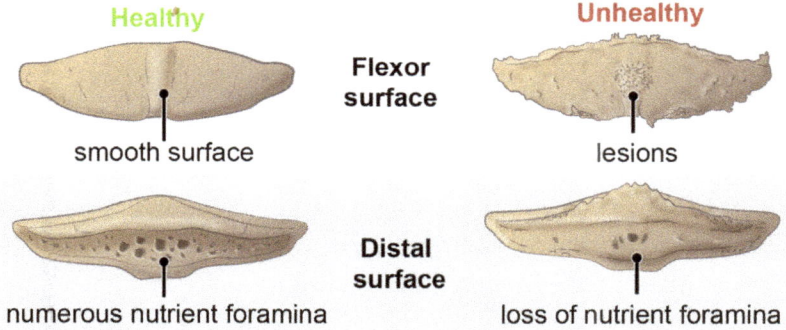

Healthy   **Unhealthy**

**Flexor
surface**

smooth surface   lesions

**Distal
surface**

numerous nutrient foramina   loss of nutrient foramina

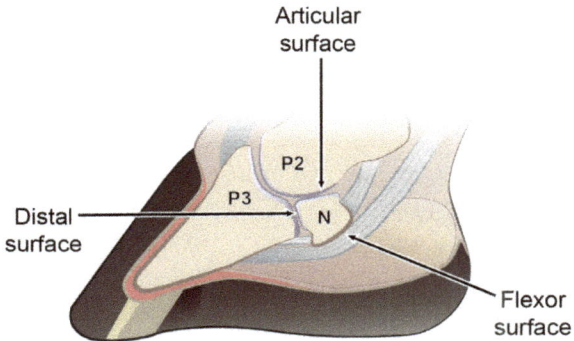

Articular
surface

P2

Distal
surface

P3

N

Flexor
surface

- **Overuse:** Navicular syndrome can also be caused by overuse or heavy use of the navicular bone. This can happen when a horse is asked to perform repetitive, intense movements on hard surfaces, such as jumping or dressage.

- **Trauma:** Trauma to the hoof or foot can also lead to navicular syndrome. A horse with a history of hoof injuries or who has experienced a severe hoof injury can make it more susceptible to developing navicular syndrome.

- **Age:** As horses age, their bones become more brittle and less elastic. The navicular bone is no exception, and as horses age, they can become more prone to developing navicular syndrome.

- **Poor quality hoof care:** Hooves that do not receive regular and adequate maintenance can be in a prolonged state of stress and imbalance, which can easily contribute to navicular disease.

Symptoms

Navicular syndrome is a condition that affects the navicular bone and the surrounding structures in the horse's hoof and causes various symptoms that can be described as generalized pain in the back half of the hoof . The most common symptoms of navicular syndrome include:

- **Lameness:** Navicular syndrome can cause lameness in the horse, especially when the horse is asked to move on hard surfaces or to make tight turns. The lameness may be more pronounced in one front foot or bilateral, affecting both front feet.

- **Pain in the heel area:** Horses with navicular syndrome may exhibit pain in the heel area when pressure is applied to the hoof. This pain can be caused by inflammation and degeneration of the navicular bone and the surrounding structures.

- **Sensitivity to hoof testers:** Hoof testers are tools used to apply pressure to different parts of the hoof to identify areas of pain. Horses with navicular syndrome may be more sensitive to hoof testers in the heel area.

- **Shortened stride:** Navicular syndrome can cause a horse to shorten its stride and appear to be "walking on its toes."
- **Hoof shape changes:** Navicular syndrome can cause changes in the shape of the hoof. The heel may appear to be contracted, and the sole may become more concave.

Diagnosis

Navicular syndrome can be a chronic and progressive condition and early diagnosis and treatment are crucial to prevent the horse from developing chronic lameness. Navicular syndrome can be complex to diagnose and related to a number of factors, so a veterinarian will typically perform a thorough physical examination and may use one or more of the following diagnostic methods:

- **Radiography (X-rays):** Radiography is an imaging technique that uses electromagnetic waves to create pictures of the internal structures of the hoof. X-rays can help identify changes in the navicular bone, such as degeneration or inflammation, which may indicate navicular syndrome.
- **Nerve blocks:** Nerve blocks involve injecting a local anesthetic into specific regions of the hoof to block pain signals. This can help identify the pain's precise location, which can help confirm a diagnosis of navicular syndrome.
- **Palpation:** A veterinarian may also use palpation to identify areas of pain or sensitivity in the hoof. They will typically apply pressure to different areas of the hoof to identify areas of pain or sensitivity.
- **Dynamic examination:** A veterinarian may also evaluate the horse while it's in motion. This can include observing the horse walking and trotting on a hard surface and asking the horse to make tight turns.
- **Blood work:** Blood work can also be performed to check for any systemic causes of lameness, such as Cushing's disease or laminitis.

Treatment

Treatment for navicular syndrome can be a long-term process and improvement may not be immediate. In some cases, even with proper treatment, navicular syndrome may progress to the point of chronic lameness, and in such cases, the horse's use may need to be re-evaluated. Treatment options for navicular syndrome will vary depending on the severity of the condition and the underlying cause and may include:

- **Rest and controlled exercise:** Rest is one of the most critical aspects of treatment for navicular syndrome. The horse should be kept in a stall or small pen and given a break from any strenuous activity such as jumping or galloping. Controlled exercise, such as hand-walking, can be introduced gradually to help maintain muscle tone and improve circulation.

- **Shoeing:** Special shoeing can help to redistribute the horse's weight and take pressure off the navicular bone. Different types of shoes, such as bar shoes or other therapeutic shoes, may be used depending on the horse's needs.

- **Medications:** Anti-inflammatory and pain-relieving medications such as phenylbutazone or firocoxib may be used to control pain and inflammation. In some cases, veterinarians may also use joint injections to reduce inflammation in the navicular area.

- **Shockwave therapy:** This non-invasive treatment uses high-energy sound waves to stimulate blood flow and healing in the affected area.

- **Surgery:** In severe cases, surgery may be required to remove the damaged portion of the navicular bone, repair the joint and/or navicular bursa.

- **Nutritional support:** Ensuring that the horse is getting the right balance of nutrients in their diet can help improve their hooves' overall health.

Prevention

Prevention methods may help in avoiding navicular syndrome, but even with proper prevention measures, navicular syndrome can still occur. Here are several steps horse owners can take to help reduce the risk of this condition developing:

- **Proper shoeing:** Proper shoeing can help to redistribute the horse's weight and take pressure off the navicular bone. Work closely with a farrier to ensure that the horse receives the appropriate type and level of support.

- **Regular farrier check-ups:** Regular farrier check-ups can help to identify and address any issues with the horse's hooves before they become a problem. A farrier should check the horse's feet for signs of wear, imbalance, or other issues contributing to navicular syndrome.

- **Avoiding overuse:** Overuse is one of the most common causes of navicular syndrome. Horse owners should avoid asking the horse to perform strenuous activities such as jumping or galloping for extended periods.

- **Proper conformation:** Proper conformation can also help prevent navicular syndrome. Horses with poor conformation may be more prone to developing this condition.

- **Proper nutrition:** Ensuring that the horse is getting the right balance of nutrients in their diet can help improve their hooves' overall health.

- **Regular veterinary check-ups:** Regular veterinary check-ups can help to identify any issues early on and prevent them from becoming more serious.

Ringbone & Sidebone

Ringbone and sidebone are common developmental orthopedic diseases (DODs) affecting the horse's distal limb. Ringbone is a degenerative condition that affects the pastern and coffin joints and is characterized by the formation of new bony growths, or exostoses, at these joints. These exostoses can cause pain, inflammation, and lameness in the affected horse. Sidebone is a degenerative condition that results in the ossification of the collateral cartilages on either side of the coffin bone. These exostoses can cause pain, inflammation, and lameness in the affected horse.

Several factors, including genetics, conformation, overuse, and injury, can cause ringbone and sidebone. Horses with poor conformation, such as those with long pasterns, low heels, and toe-in or toe-out, are more susceptible to ringbone and sidebone than horses with good conformation. Overuse and injury can also cause ringbone and sidebone by putting excessive stress on the joints and bones.

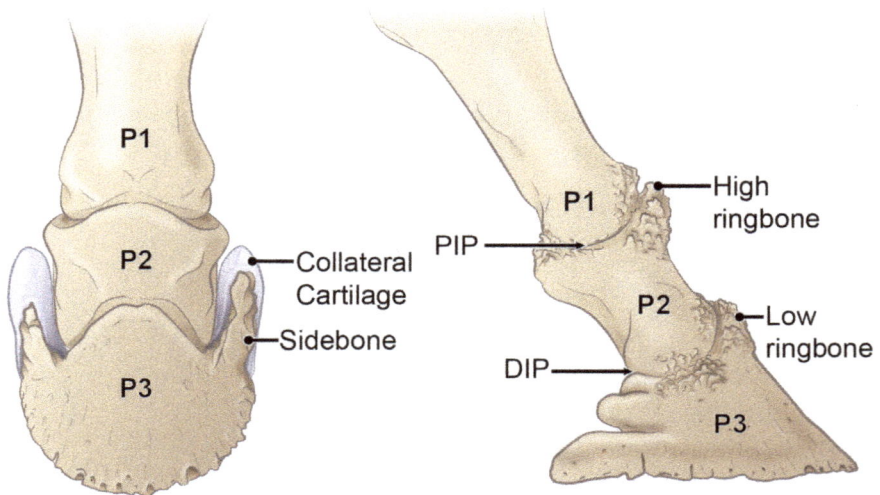

Symptoms

Ringbone and sidebone are both terms used to describe bony growths that occur in the pastern or coffin joints of a horse's distal limb. The horse may have difficulty flexing or extending the joint, and there may be visible swelling or bony growths. The horse may also exhibit a short, choppy gait and may be reluctant to move. In severe cases, the horse may be unable to bear weight on the affected limb.

Symptoms of ringbone include:

- Lameness, which may be mild to severe, and may be present in one or multiple limbs.

- Swelling and heat in the affected joint.

- Pain when the joint is palpated or when the horse is flexed.

- Stiffness and reluctance to move the affected limb.

- Changes in hoof shape, such as a dropped sole or flared walls.

Symptoms of sidebone include:

- Lameness, which may be mild to severe, and may be present in one or multiple limbs.

- Swelling and heat in the affected joint.

- Pain when the joint is palpated or when the horse is flexed.

- Stiffness and reluctance to move the affected limb.

- Bony enlargements on the inside or outside of the affected joint, which may or may not be accompanied by lameness.

Diagnosis

Ringbone and sidebone are both bony growths that can occur in the distal limb of a horse, and they are typically diagnosed through a combination of physical examination and diagnostic imaging. It is important to note that the symptoms of ringbone and sidebone can be similar to other conditions, and a veterinarian should be consulted for proper diagnosis and treatment.

- **Physical examination:** The veterinarian will likely start by performing a thorough physical examination of the horse's distal limb, including palpation of the affected area to feel for any bony growths or heat. They may also observe the horse moving, looking for any signs of lameness or stiffness.

- **Radiography:** Radiography, also known as x-ray, is a common method for diagnosing ringbone and sidebone. Radiographs will show the bony growths, and can help the veterinarian determine their size and location.

- **Ultrasonography:** Ultrasonography can be used to visualize the soft tissue surrounding the bony growths, which can help the veterinarian determine the extent of the condition and how it is affecting the horse.

- **Nuclear Scintigraphy:** Nuclear scintigraphy, also known as bone scanning, is a technique that uses a small amount of radioactive material and a special camera to create detailed images of the bones. This method is useful in detecting and assessing bone changes, including ringbone and sidebone.

- **Magnetic Resonance Imaging (MRI):** MRI is a diagnostic tool that uses a magnetic field and radio waves to create detailed images of the horse's distal limb, including the bones, tendons and ligaments. This method can be useful in identifying soft tissue changes that may be contributing to the development of ringbone and sidebone.

- **Computed Tomography (CT):** CT scans use a combination of x-rays and computer technology to create detailed images of the horse's distal limb, including the bones, tendons, ligaments and soft tissue. This method can be useful in identifying bony growths such as ringbone and sidebone, as well as any other abnormalities in the distal limb.

Treatment

Treatment for ringbone and sidebone typically involves managing the pain and inflammation in the joint. While these conditions may be managed and treated, they cannot be cured, and the horse may need to be managed for the rest of its life. Common treatment options include:

- **Rest and Controlled Exercise:** Rest is one of the most important aspects of treating ringbone and sidebone. This can be achieved by reducing the horse's workload and limiting its time spent in the stable. Controlled exercise can also be used to help reduce inflammation and pain.

- **Cold Therapy:** Cold therapy is often used to help reduce inflammation and pain associated with ringbone and sidebone. Cold therapy can be achieved by using ice packs, cold water hosing, or cold compresses.

- **Medications:** Non-steroidal anti-inflammatory drugs (NSAIDs) such as phenylbutazone or firocoxib are commonly used to help reduce pain and inflammation associated with ringbone and sidebone.

- **Shoeing and Orthotics:** Shoeing and orthotics can be used to help redistribute weight away from affected areas and provide additional support to the hoof. Close management and communication with your farrier is essential.

- **Joint Injections:** Joint injections can be used to help reduce inflammation and pain in the affected joint. Commonly used medications include hyaluronic acid, corticosteroids, and polysulfated glycosaminoglycans.

- **Surgery:** In severe cases, surgery may be needed to remove or repair damaged tissue, or to permanently fuse the affected joint.

- **Rehabilitation:** Physical therapy and rehabilitation exercises may be used to help improve joint mobility and strength, as well as to help prevent recurrence of ringbone and sidebone.

- **Nutrition:** Proper nutrition is important to support healthy joint function; it's recommended to provide the horse with a balanced diet with the proper amounts of vitamins and minerals, particularly those that support joint health.

- **Acupuncture and Chiropractic Care:** Acupuncture and chiropractic care can be used to help reduce pain and inflammation and improve joint function.

Prevention

Preventing ringbone and sidebone in horses involves a combination of proper management, regular hoof care, and addressing any underlying issues that may be contributing to the development of these conditions. Some key methods of prevention include:

- **Regular farrier care:** Scheduling regular farrier visits to have your horse's hooves trimmed and shod can help prevent ringbone and sidebone by ensuring that the hooves are properly balanced and that any issues are identified and addressed early on.

- **Proper nutrition:** Feeding your horse a balanced diet that includes the proper amounts of protein, vitamins, and minerals can help keep the hooves healthy and strong, reducing the risk of ringbone and sidebone.

- **Adequate exercise:** Exercise is important for maintaining overall health, including hoof health, so providing your horse with regular opportunities to move and stretch can help prevent ringbone and sidebone.

- **Proper footing:** Maintaining safe and appropriate footing in your horse's stall and turnout areas can help prevent ringbone and sidebone by reducing the risk of slips, falls, and other injuries.

- **Management of underlying conditions:** If your horse has underlying conditions such as laminitis or navicular disease, it's important to work with your veterinarian to manage these conditions and prevent ringbone and sidebone from developing.

- **Regular monitoring:** Keeping a close eye on your horse's hooves and legs and noting any changes in conformation or gait can help you identify ringbone and sidebone early on and take steps to prevent them.

- **Use of supportive devices:** Supportive devices such as boots can be used to help prevent ringbone and sidebone by providing extra support and cushioning for the hoof.

- **Proper shoeing:** Proper shoeing can help prevent ringbone and sidebone by ensuring that the hoof is well-supported and that the horse is able to move comfortably.

- **Avoid overuse:** Overuse of the horse's legs can lead to ringbone and sidebone, so it's important to avoid overworking your horse and to give him adequate rest and recovery time.

- **Weight Management:** Maintaining a healthy weight for your horse can help prevent ringbone and sidebone by reducing the stress on the horse's legs and hooves.

Acute Injury

Acute injuries refer to sudden and severe injuries to the horse's hoof or limb, such as punctures, lacerations, fractures, sprains and strains These injuries can cause pain, swelling, and lameness and can lead to serious complications if left untreated.

Acute hoof injuries can occur from a variety of causes, such as stepping on a sharp object, being kicked by another horse, or landing on a hard surface. These injuries can cause damage to the sensitive structures within the hoof, such as the sensitive laminae, the digital cushion, or the hoof wall.

Soft tissue injuries in the distal limb of horses can vary in severity and type, ranging from mild strains to severe tears or ruptures. These injuries can affect various structures, including tendons, ligaments, muscles, and other soft tissues surrounding the joints. Here are some common types of soft tissue injuries in the distal limb of horses:

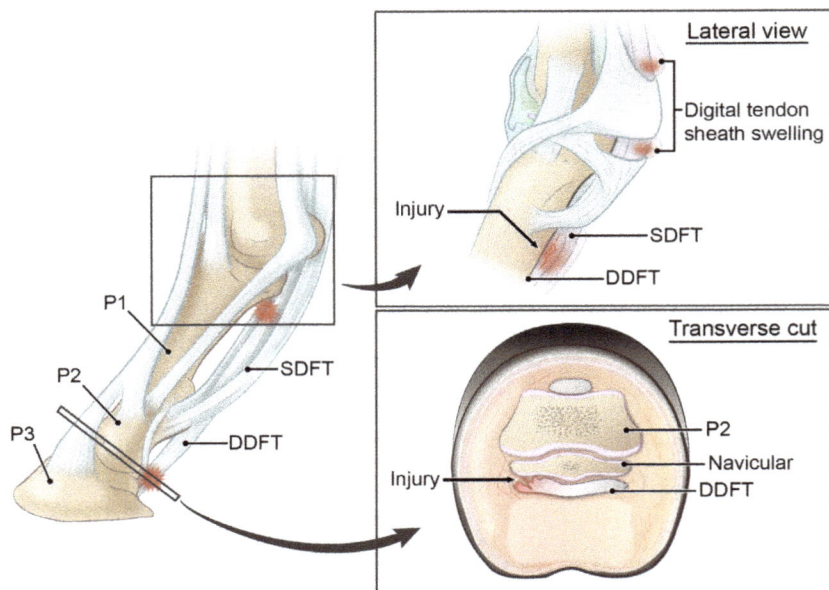

■ **Tendon Injuries:**

• **Tendonitis:** Inflammation of the tendon, which can result from overuse, trauma, or poor conformation. It may present with heat, swelling, and lameness.

• **Tendon Tears or Ruptures:** Partial or complete tears of the tendon fibers, often resulting from excessive strain or trauma. Severe cases may cause significant lameness and swelling.

• **Tendinopathy:** Degenerative changes within the tendon due to repetitive strain or aging, leading to reduced elasticity and increased risk of injury.

■ **Ligament Injuries:**

• **Sprains:** Stretching or tearing of ligament fibers, commonly occurring due to sudden movements, slips, or falls. Ligament sprains can range from mild to severe, affecting joint stability and function.

• **Desmitis:** Inflammation of a ligament, often caused by

repetitive stress or trauma. Desmitis can result in lameness, heat, and swelling around the affected area.

■ Muscle Injuries:

- **Strains:** Overstretching or tearing of muscle fibers, typically caused by sudden movements, excessive exertion, or trauma. Muscle strains can vary in severity, leading to lameness, swelling, and discomfort.

- **Contusions:** Bruising of muscle tissue due to direct trauma or impact. While usually not serious, severe contusions can cause pain, swelling, and lameness.

■ Joint Injuries:

- **Synovitis:** Inflammation of the synovial membrane lining the joint capsule, often resulting from infection, trauma, or repetitive stress. Synovitis can lead to joint effusion, lameness, and discomfort.

- **Capsulitis:** Inflammation of the joint capsule, typically caused by trauma, overuse, or conformational abnormalities. Capsulitis can affect joint stability and range of motion.

■ Soft Tissue Hematomas:

- Accumulation of blood within soft tissues due to trauma, contusions, or vascular injury. Hematomas can cause swelling, pain, and lameness, depending on their size and location.

■ Subcutaneous and Deep Tissue Injuries:

- **Lacerations:** Cuts or tears in the skin and underlying tissues, often resulting from trauma or sharp objects. Proper wound care is essential to prevent infection and promote healing.

- **Avulsions:** Avulsion occurs when there is a partial or complete tearing away of the skin and the tissue beneath. Avulsions typically occur during violent accidents.

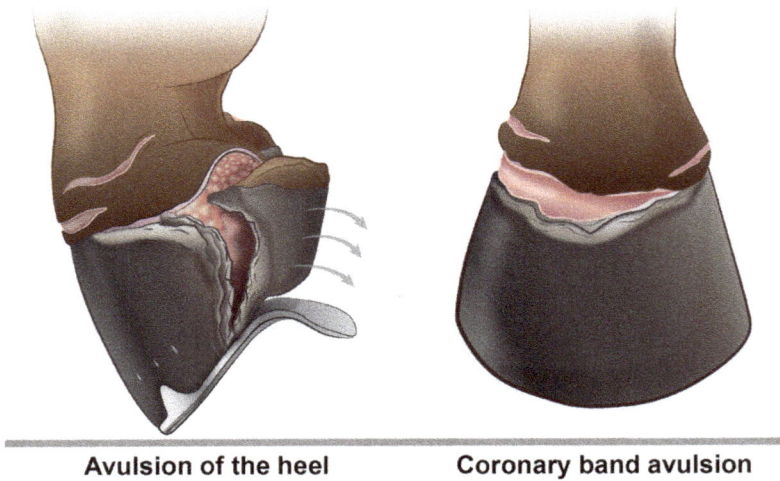

Avulsion of the heel   **Coronary band avulsion**

Treatment for soft tissue injuries in horses typically involves rest, anti-inflammatory medication, physical therapy, and sometimes surgical intervention, depending on the severity and type of injury. Proper veterinary evaluation and management are essential to ensure optimal healing and minimize long-term complications.

Symptoms

Symptoms of acute hoof injuries can include severe lameness, pain, swelling, and heat in the affected hoof or limb, and can also cause the horse to be sensitive to the touch or when the foot is being picked up. In more severe cases, the horse may not be able to bear weight on the affected limb at all.

The symptoms of an acute injury can vary depending on the type and severity of the injury, but generally, they include the following:

- **Severe lameness:** The horse may be reluctant to put weight on the affected hoof and may have an abnormal gait.

- **Pain or sensitivity:** The horse may be sensitive to the touch or when picking up the affected limb. The horse may respond to hoof testers or may flinch when the hoof or limb is handled.

- **Swelling:** The affected hoof or joint may be swollen and warm to the touch.
- **Heat:** The affected area may be warmer than the others, indicating inflammation.
- **Bruising or bleeding:** There may be visible bruising or bleeding from the affected area.
- **Discharge:** Pus or other discharge may be present if there is an infection.
- **Digital pulse:** The pulse in the affected limb may be increased. Pulse rate or respiration rate may also be increased.

Diagnosis

The veterinarian will conduct a physical examination and may use diagnostic tools such as x-rays, ultrasound, or MRI to determine the extent of the injury and design an appropriate treatment plan. The methods of diagnosing an acute hoof injury can include the following:

- **Physical examination:** The veterinarian will conduct a thorough physical inspection of the affected hoof and limb, looking for signs of pain, swelling, heat, and sensitivity. They may also use hoof testers to check for pain or sensitivity in specific areas of the hoof.
- **Radiography (x-rays):** Radiographs can identify fractures, dislocations, or other structural abnormalities within the hoof.
- **Ultrasound:** Ultrasound can be used to evaluate the soft tissue structures within the hoof, such as the digital cushion, and detect injuries, such as tendon or ligament tears.
- **Nuclear scintigraphy:** Nuclear scintigraphy (bone scan) can identify areas of increased activity within the hoof that may indicate an injury or infection.
- **Magnetic Resonance Imaging (MRI):** MRI can be used to evaluate the internal structures of the foot and limb, such as the digital cushion and the navicular bone.

■ **Blood tests:** Blood tests can detect signs of infection or inflammation and rule out other conditions that may be causing lameness.

Treatment

The specific treatment plan will depend on the type and severity of the injury and the overall health of the horse. It's important to follow the veterinarian's instructions and provide proper care and management during recovery to ensure the best outcome. The horse must be kept in a clean and dry environment and given adequate rest and time to heal. Regular follow-up appointments with the veterinarian may be needed to monitor the healing progress and make necessary adjustments to the treatment plan. The methods of treating an acute hoof injury can include:

■ **Pain management:** The horse will be given pain medication to alleviate pain and discomfort.

■ **Wound care:** The affected area will be cleaned, and debris or foreign bodies will be removed. The wound will be dressed with a suitable bandage and medication to help prevent infection and promote healing.

■ **Immobilization:** The affected limb may be placed in a cast or splint to immobilize the hoof and prevent further damage.

■ **Cold therapy:** Cold therapy can reduce inflammation and swelling in the affected area.

■ **Supportive shoeing:** The horse may be fitted with a particular shoe or pad to provide additional support and protection to the affected hoof.

■ **Physical therapy:** Physical therapy may help the horse regain strength and range of motion in the affected limb.

■ **Antibiotics:** If there is an infection, antibiotics will be given to clear it up.

■ **Surgery:** In some cases, surgery may be necessary to repair the damage.

Prevention

Taking preventative measures can help reduce the risk of hoof injuries and ensure your horse's hooves stay healthy and strong. The methods of preventing acute hoof injuries can include:

- **Regular hoof care:** Regular hoof care, including trimming and shoeing, can help keep the hooves in good condition and prevent problems such as overgrown hooves, which can lead to injuries.

- **Proper nutrition:** Proper nutrition is essential for hoof health. A diet rich in essential nutrients, such as biotin, zinc, and copper, can help promote strong and healthy hooves.

- **Proper stall and pasture management:** Providing a clean and dry environment for your horse can help prevent hoof injuries caused by wet or muddy conditions, as well as injuries from debris and foreign objects.

- **Regular exercise and turnout:** Regular exercise and turnout can help keep your horse's hooves in good condition and prevent injuries caused by prolonged periods of inactivity.

- **Regular veterinary check-ups:** Regular veterinary check-ups can help detect potential hoof problems early on before they become more serious.

- **Proper shoeing:** Proper shoeing can help protect the hooves and provide additional support and traction, which can help prevent injuries.

- **Avoiding overuse:** Overuse is one of the significant causes of distal limb injuries, so it's important to avoid overworking your horse and to provide appropriate rest and recovery time after intense exercise or activity.

- **Monitoring your horse's weight:** Obesity is a major risk factor for serious hoof disorders, so it's important to monitor your horse's weight and ensure they are healthy.

- **Proper training and handling:** Proper training and handling can help to reduce the animal's fear and stress which can dramatically reduce the risk of injury.

First Aid

F IRST AID AIMS TO PREVENT FURTHER HARM and promote recovery by addressing any immediate life-threatening conditions, controlling bleeding, providing pain relief, and preventing infection. Anyone with basic knowledge and training can perform first aid. It can include various techniques, such bandaging and medicating wounds, splinting broken bones, and administering medication. Horse owners must have a basic understanding of first aid to provide immediate care to their horses in case of injury or illness and know when to seek professional help.

First aid for hoof and distal limb injuries and conditions is essential for horse owners to understand for several reasons. One of the primary reasons is that these types of injuries and conditions can cause severe pain and discomfort to the horse, and prompt treatment can help alleviate this pain and prevent further damage. Additionally, many hoof and distal limb injuries and conditions can have long-term effects on the horse's overall health and mobility, and early intervention can help prevent these adverse outcomes.

Another reason why first aid for hoof and distal limb injuries and conditions is essential for horse owners to understand is that many of these injuries and conditions can be quite common, and horse owners should be prepared to recognize and address them in the event that they occur. For example, horses are prone to hoof abscesses, puncture wounds, and laminitis, all of which can be treated with appropriate and timely first aid.

Furthermore, knowing first aid for hoof and distal limb injuries and conditions can help horse owners better communicate with farriers, veterinarians, and other equine professionals. Horse owners who can recognize and report symptoms of hoof and distal limb injuries and conditions can help these professionals diagnose and treat the issue more efficiently.

First Aid Kit

A complete and effective first aid kit for treating hoof and distal limb injuries or conditions should include the following items:

- **Hoof pick:** This tool is used for cleaning out debris from the hoof, such as stones or mud, and is essential for treating abscesses or puncture wounds.

- **Rectal Thermometer:** This is used for measuring the horse's temperature, which can indicate an infection or other condition.

- **Scissors:** These are used for cutting and trimming bandages and other materials used in first aid treatment.

- **Tweezers:** These are used for removing any foreign objects that may be stuck in the hoof, such as nails or thorns.

- **Disinfectant spray or solution:** This is used for cleaning and disinfecting any wounds or injuries before dressing them. Betadine or chlorhexidine.

- **Non-adhesive bandages:** These are used for covering and protecting wounds and can be wrapped around the hoof to provide support.

- **Gauze pads:** These are used for covering minor cuts and wounds and can be used to provide padding for sensitive feet.

- **Elastic bandage:** This is used to provide support and compression to the distal limb and can treat injuries such as sprains or strains.

- **Duct tape:** Thick, strong tape can be used to secure bandages and padding to the hoof and prevent premature wear on the bandage.

- **Cold pack:** This can reduce inflammation and pain in the distal limb and can be applied to the hoof or leg.

- **Hoof pads:** This is used for providing additional cushioning and support to the hoof and can be used for treating conditions such as laminitis.

- **Hoof packing:** This is used for filling gaps or voids in the hoof and can be used for treating abscesses or other injuries.

- **Hoof boot:** This is used for protecting the hoof and providing support when the horse is walking or standing.

- **Hoof trimming tools:** Nippers, hoof knives, and rasps can be useful for addressing overgrown hooves and damaged hoof wall, removing pressure points that can cause further pain or injury.

- **Shoe pulling tools:** A clinch cutter, shoe puller, and crease nail pullers can make removing a damaged shoe much easier.

- **Hoof tester:** This tool is used for detecting sensitivity in the hoof, which can indicate an abscess or other injury.

- **Hoof stand:** This is used for holding the horse's hoof in place while treating it and is much easier than supporting the horse's weight with your body.

- **Hoof care guide or manual:** This provides instruction and guidance on how to treat hoof and distal limb injuries and conditions.

Checking Vitals

Checking a horse's vital signs is an important aspect of horse care, as it allows the owner to monitor the overall health and well-being of their horse. The vital signs that are typically checked include temperature, pulse, respiration, and capillary refill time (CRT).

- **Temperature:** The normal temperature for a horse is between 98°F and 101.5°F. A temperature that is significantly higher than this range could indicate a fever, which is a sign of an underlying infection or inflammation. To take a horse's temperature, a rectal thermometer should be lubricated with petroleum jelly and inserted into the horse's rectum. The thermometer should be left in place for at least one minute to ensure an accurate reading. A digital thermometer will beep when reading is ready.

■ **Pulse:** The normal resting heart rate for a horse is between 28 and 44 beats per minute. A heart rate that is significantly higher or lower than this range could indicate a problem, such as anemia, heart disease, or stress. To take a horse's pulse, the owner should place their hand on the horse's facial artery, which is located just below the jawbone on the left side of the horse's head. The owner should count the number of beats for 15 seconds and then multiply that number by four to obtain the horse's heart rate per minute. Alternatively, you may check the digital pulse at the digital artery along the fetlock. A strong, bounding digital pulse may be an indicator of laminitis or an infection in the hoof.

■ **Respiration:** The normal breathing rate for a horse at rest is between 8 and 16 breaths per minute. A respiratory rate that is significantly higher than this range could indicate a respiratory issue, such as pneumonia, or a systemic issue, such as fever or pain. To check a horse's respiration, the owner should observe the horse's nostrils and count the number of times they flare in one minute.

■ **Capillary Refill Time (CRT):** Capillary refill time is a measure of the time it takes for blood to refill the capillaries after being pressed on. Normal CRT for a horse is around 1-2 seconds. Abnormal capillary refill time can indicate several things in a horse, including poor circulation, dehydration, shock, or heart and cardiovascular

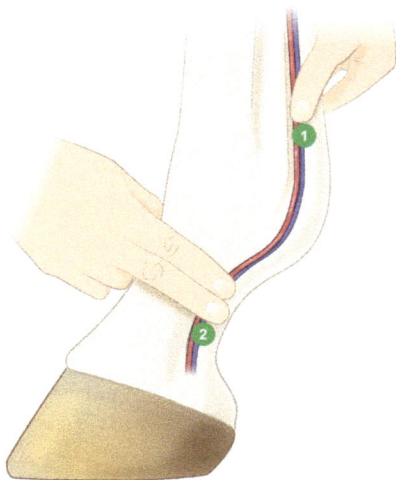

problems. To check a horse's CRT, the owner should press their thumb onto the horse's gums, in the area where the gums meet the teeth, and release. The time it takes for the gums to turn from white back to pink is the CRT.

Other vital signs that may be checked include hydration, gut sounds, and muscle tone. To check for hydration, the owner should observe the horse's eyes, skin, and gums and assess for any signs of dehydration, such as sunken eyes, dry skin, or sticky gums. To check for gut sounds, the owner should place their ear against the horse's side and listen for any sounds of digestion. To check for muscle tone, the owner should observe the horse's muscles and assess for any signs of atrophy or weakness.

While these are the standard vital signs to check, they are only a snapshot of the horse's overall health and should be used in conjunction with other diagnostic methods such as blood tests, radiographs, and ultrasound. It is also important to establish a baseline of these vital signs for your horse and to monitor them regularly to detect any changes that may indicate a problem. A veterinarian should be consulted if any abnormal vital signs are detected.

Using Hoof Testers

Hoof testers are used to help identify areas of pain in a horse's hoof, and can be a valuable tool in assessing the overall health of the hoof. The process of using hoof testers involves applying pressure to different areas of the hoof to identify any painful or sensitive spots. By using hoof testers, you can help identify potential problems with your horse's hooves, such as laminitis, abscesses, or other painful hoof conditions. Regular use of hoof testers can also help you track the progress of any hoof issues that are being treated, and can provide valuable information to your farrier or veterinarian.

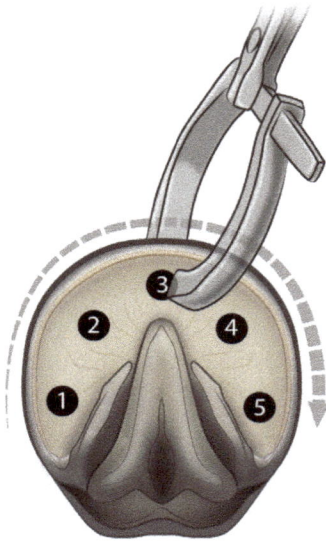

Sole

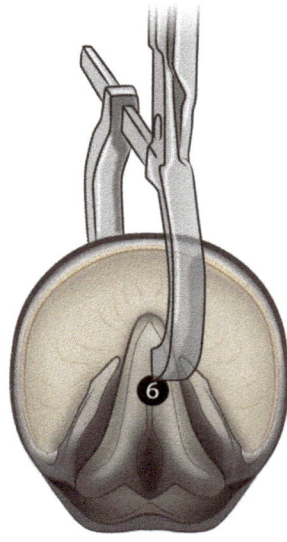

Center of frog

Sides of frog

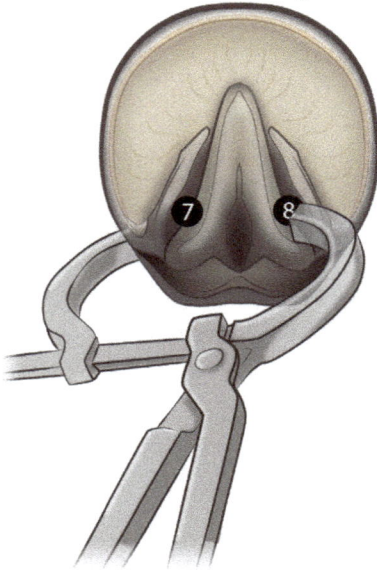

Across the heels

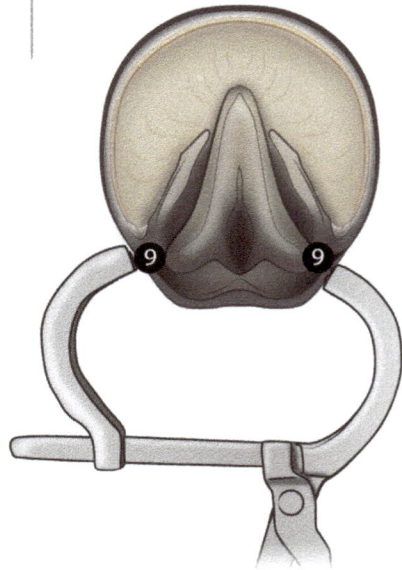

Here is a step-by-step process for using hoof testers:

1. **Clean the hoof:** Before using hoof testers, make sure that the hoof is clean and free of any debris. Use a hoof pick to remove any dirt or stones from the sole and frog of the hoof.

2. **Prepare the hoof testers:** Hoof testers come in a variety of sizes and styles, so it's important to choose the right one for the size and shape of your horse's hoof. Ensure that the testers are clean and free from any rust or sharp edges that could cause injury.

3. **Position the horse:** Stand on the side of the horse where you will be testing, and hold the horse's hoof between your knees or with your off hand. Have the horse restrained in ties or held by an assistant.

4. **Apply pressure:** Start by applying light pressure to different areas of the hoof with the hoof testers. In each spot, gradually increase pressure (imagine your squeeze on a range of 0 to 5) and pay close attention to the horse's reaction, looking for any signs of discomfort or pain. Start at the outer edge of the hoof and move the testers in a circular pattern, testing the wall, sole, frog, and heels. Start your test on a hoof and location where you do not expect to find a problem so you can establish a baseline reaction for your horse.

5. **Record the results:** Record the areas of the hoof that were sensitive when pressure was applied. Take note of the location and level of sensitivity for each area, as this information can be valuable for your farrier or veterinarian when making a diagnosis.

6. **Repeat:** Repeat the same process for the other three hooves, testing each hoof in the same manner as the first.

7. **Shock test:** Additionally, you can tap around the hoof with a hammer or other tool to test for sensitivity to concussion, which may not be easily identified with the gradual squeeze of hoof testers.

Treatment Protocols

Horses have surprisingly delicate anatomy for such a large and powerful animal. Unfortunately, injuries and damage are often a question of when, not if. Being equipped with knowledge and adequate tools will prepare you take charge when your horse is at risk, saving your horse from unnecessary pain and reducing emergency veterinary bills. In this section, you will find step-by-step instructions on handling some common hoof-related injuries and conditions.

Pulling a Shoe

If your horse wears shoes, there will inevitably come a time when a shoe becomes damaged. Horses find many unique ways to pull shoes, from tromping through mud, hooking fences, or stepping on themselves. In some instances the shoe may become loose, damaged, or bent, but remain attached to the hoof. Removing the shoe as soon as possible can prevent injury or further damage to the hoof.

Pulling a horseshoe can be a difficult process for someone who is not trained or experienced, but with some simple tools and patience, you can pull a shoe to protect your horse's hoof from further damage. Watch your farrier the next time they pull shoes off your horse, or ask your farrier to teach you how to pull a shoe in case of emergencies. Here is a step-by-step guide on how to pull a horseshoe:

1. **Gather all necessary tools:** Before starting the process, have all the necessary tools within reach. Professional tools make the job much easier: mallet and clinch cutter (or a rasp), shoe puller, and crease nail pullers. If these tools are not available, the job can be done with a hammer, flathead screwdriver or dull wood chisel, and pliers.

2. **Prepare the horse:** Before starting, make sure the horse is calm and secure. Have the horse tied in a safe location with solid, level footing. If necessary, have a second person assist in holding the horse still.

3. **Assess the shoe:** Look at the shoe and the hoof to determine how the shoe is attached and how best to remove it. Check for any cracks or damaged hoof wall from torn nails. Make a note of how many nails will need to be removed, as some can be hard to see if the hoof is dirty.

4. **Cut the clinches:** The end of each nail is bent over to form a hook that keeps the shoe secured to the hoof. This crimp in the nail is known as the "clinch." Pull the foot forward and brace it on a hoof stand or the top of your thigh. Using a mallet and clinch cutter, or hammer and flathead screwdriver (or dull wood chisel), tap and pry the clinch upward to straighten the nail. This will prevent further damage to the hoof wall when the shoe is pulled. Alternatively, you can use the finer side of a farrier's rasp to file the clinches off.

5. **Pull the shoe:** Once the clinches are cut, pull the foot up to the rear and brace the hoof between your knees. Using a shoe puller, grab the shoe at the heel, behind the last nail, and push the shoe puller sharply down towards the toe. Repeat on the opposite heel. If the shoe does not easily come off, tap the shoe back down onto the hoof and remove each nail with the shoe puller or crease nail pullers. If these tools are not available, you can pry the shoe up with your flathead screwdriver, chisel, or the claw of a hammer. Then, tap the shoe back down to the hoof and pull the exposed nails with a pair of pliers.

6. **Protect the hoof:** Once the shoe is removed, clean the hoof and check for any damage. Wrap the hoof in a layer of Vetrap and duct tape to prevent further damage to the hoof wall until your farrier can return to replace the shoe.

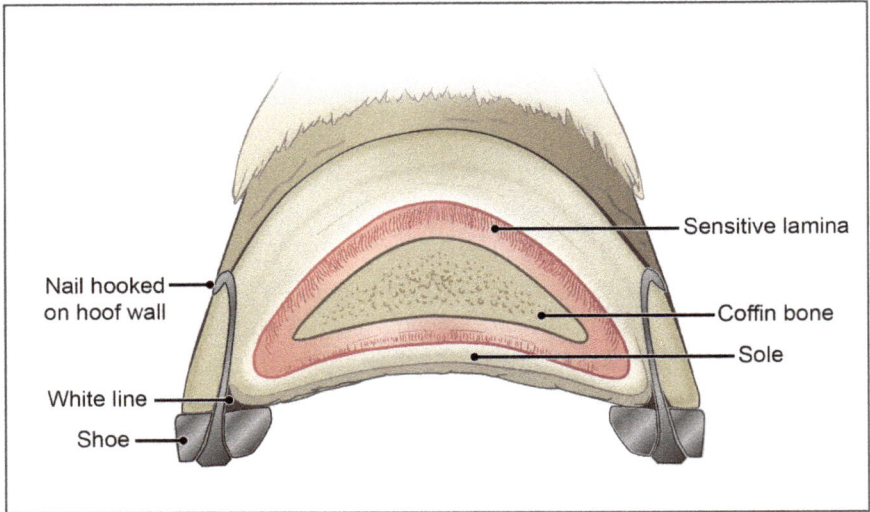

Sensitive lamina

Nail hooked on hoof wall

Coffin bone

Sole

White line

Shoe

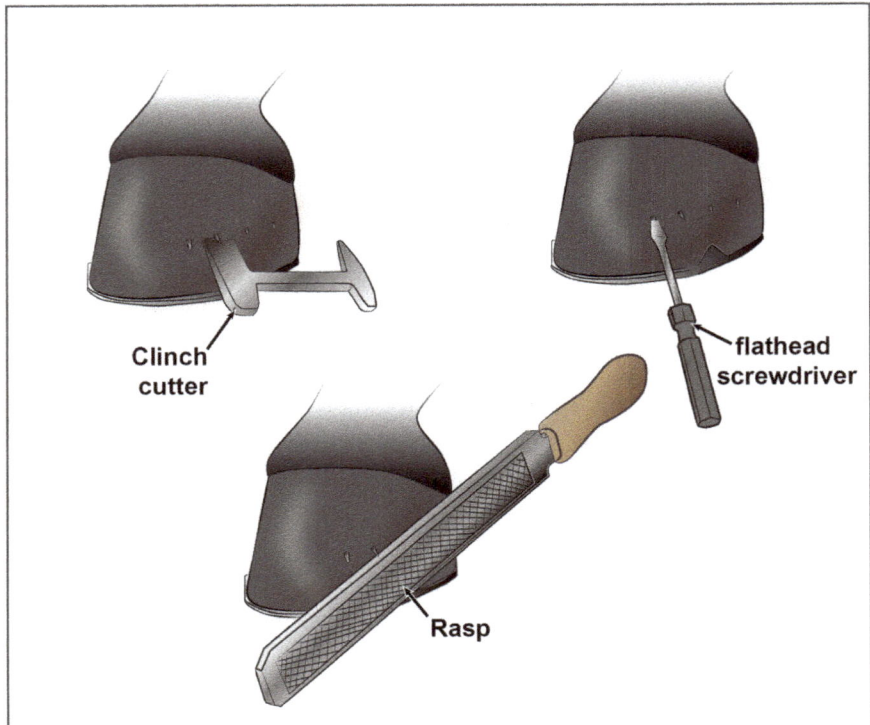

Clinch cutter

flathead screwdriver

Rasp

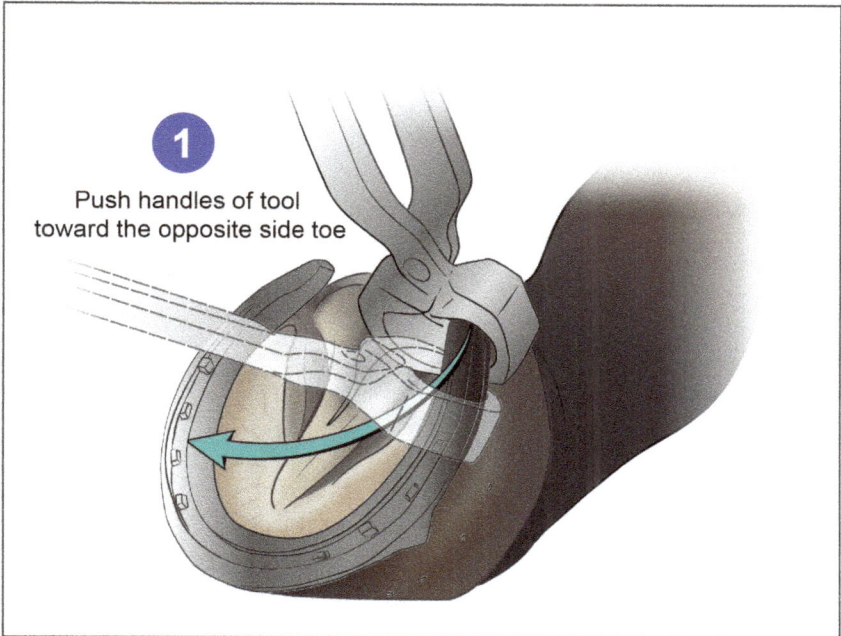

1 Push handles of tool toward the opposite side toe

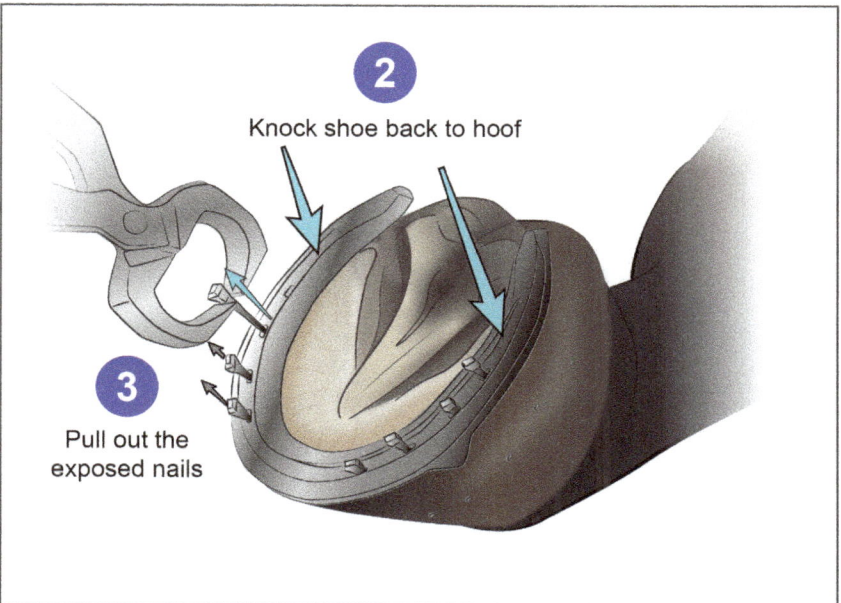

2 Knock shoe back to hoof

3 Pull out the exposed nails

Lost Shoe

If your horse has lost a shoe completely, wrap the hoof as in step 6 above and contact your farrier. If the shoe was lost in a stall or pasture, make your best effort to find the shoe. A lost, damaged shoe and nails can be hazardous and result in injury if the horse steps on it. Additionally, your farrier may be able to replace the same shoe and the damage to the shoe can help the farrier identify how it was lost.

Abscess Treatment

When a horse has a hoof abscess, addressing the issue as quickly as possible can relieve pain, prevent further complications and promote healing. Here is a step-by-step guide for administering first aid to a horse with a hoof abscess:

1. **Restrain the horse:** Have someone hold the horse securely while you tend to the abscess. This will ensure the safety of both the horse and the person administering first aid.

2. **Clean the area:** Using a hoof pick or stiff brush, gently clean the entire sole and the area around the abscess. This will help to remove any debris or dirt that may obscure view of the abscess.

3. **Locate the abscess:** The abscess may not be easily observed on the sole unless it is very near the surface or already draining. Look for black sludge, blood, or puss discharge. An abscess may blow-out and drain further up the hoof near the coronary band.

4. **Do not puncture the abscess:** If the abscess has not yet drained, do not attempt to puncture the abscess. You may end up invading the tissue too deeply, creating a larger wound that will require more intense treatment.

5. **Flush the abscess:** Use clean water to flush the abscess. This will help to remove any remaining debris and bacteria. You may also soak the foot, using a bucket or soaker boot, in an epsom salt bath. This will help to soothe the foot and draw out remaining infection.

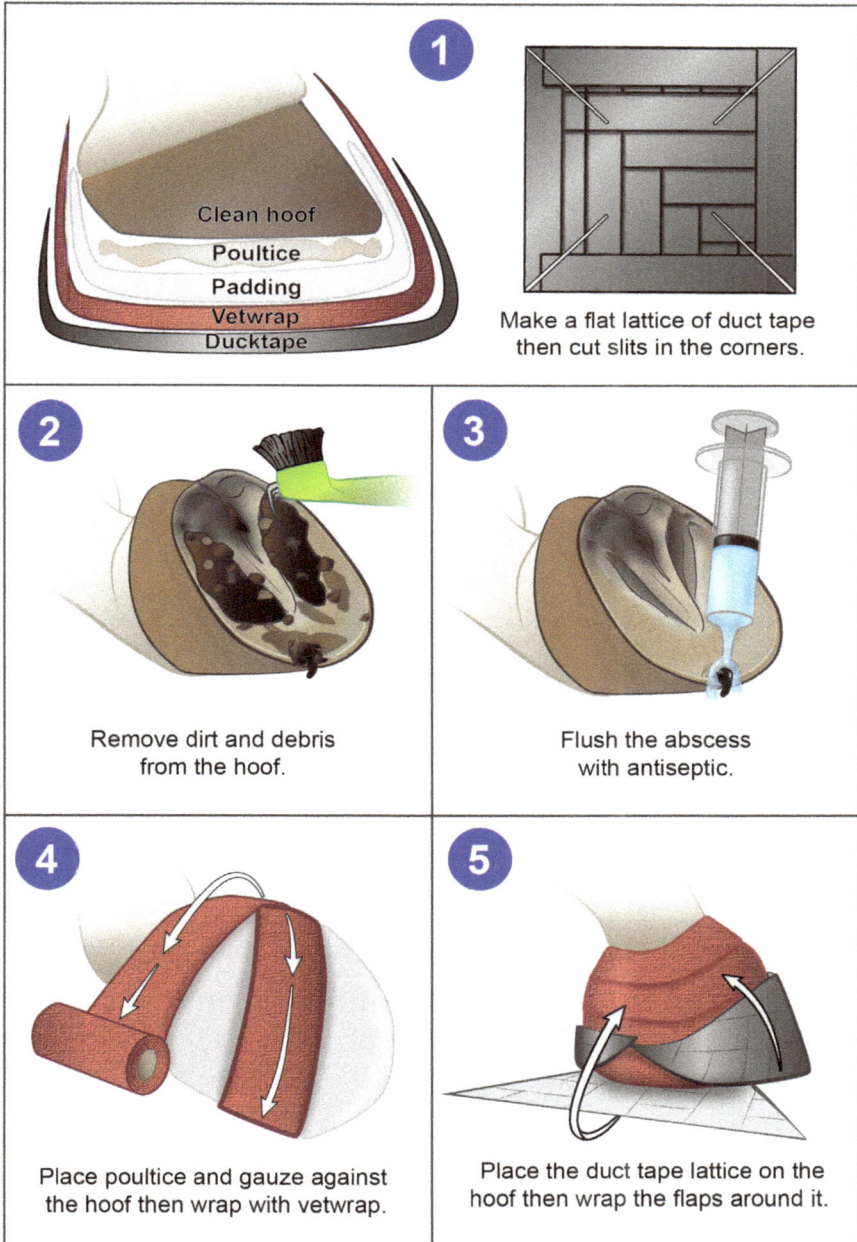

1

Clean hoof
Poultice
Padding
Vetwrap
Ducktape

Make a flat lattice of duct tape
then cut slits in the corners.

2

Remove dirt and debris
from the hoof.

3

Flush the abscess
with antiseptic.

4

Place poultice and gauze against
the hoof then wrap with vetwrap.

5

Place the duct tape lattice on the
hoof then wrap the flaps around it.

6. **Apply an antiseptic:** After flushing the abscess, apply an antiseptic solution such as iodine or chlorhexidine to the area, or the entire sole, to help prevent further infection.

7. **Bandage the hoof:** Using gauze, hoof pads, or a disposable diaper, apply a poultice or hoof packing to the sole of the hoof. Wrap the hoof with a layer of Vetrap or Elastikon tape and several layer of duct tape. Make sure the bandage is not too tight, as this can inhibit blood flow to the area. Avoid bandaging above the hairline.

8. **Monitor the horse:** Keep an eye on the horse and monitor the abscess for any signs of worsening or improvement.

Acute Laminitis Treatment

Acute laminitis is a serious condition that requires immediate attention and proper care. The following is a step-by-step guide for administering first aid to a horse suffering from acute laminitis:

1. **Contact a veterinarian immediately:** Acute laminitis requires professional medical attention and should be treated by a veterinarian as soon as possible.

2. **Keep the horse calm and reduce its movement:** Laminitis causes severe pain and discomfort, so keeping the horse calm and minimizing its movement is crucial to prevent further damage.

3. **Provide supportive care:** This includes providing the horse with a comfortable place stand or to lie down with lots of padding or deep bedding material. Provide easy access to food and water.

4. **Cold therapy:** Cold therapy is often used to reduce inflammation and pain in horses with laminitis. Apply a cold pack, ice, or cold water to the affected hooves to help reduce inflammation and pain. In many cases, swift application of cold therapy is the key to preventing coffin bone rotation.

5. **Administer pain medication:** Non-steroidal anti-inflammatory drugs (NSAIDs) such as phenylbutazone or flunixin meglumine can be used to manage pain and inflammation.

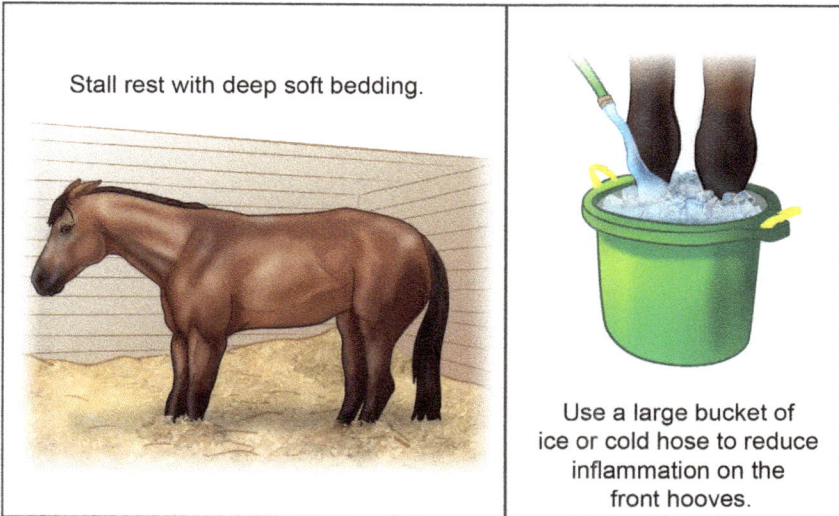

Stall rest with deep soft bedding.

Use a large bucket of ice or cold hose to reduce inflammation on the front hooves.

6. **Monitor the horse's vital signs:** Keep a close eye on the horse's vital signs, such as its heart rate, respiratory rate, and temperature, to ensure that it remains stable.

7. **Monitor the horse's response to treatment:** Observe the horse's response to treatment and inform the veterinarian of any changes in its condition.

It is important to remember that laminitis is a severe condition that can have long-term effects on a horse's health and well-being. Therefore, it is vital to seek professional medical attention as soon as possible and to follow the veterinarian's instructions for care and treatment.

Puncture Wound Treatment

Administering first aid to a horse with a puncture wound in its hoof requires a few basic steps, which should be carried out with care and caution.

1. **Assess the wound:** The first step is carefully examining the injury to determine its size, depth, and location. This will help you determine the appropriate course of treatment.

1 Clean the hoof of dirt and debris, and wash with a mild antiseptic solution.

2 Take pictures of the location and orientation of the object.

If the object is small or likely to cause further insertion if left in place, remove the object.

3

For larger objects that are secure in place or likely penetrating a joint/bone, pad the object and wait for veterinary assistance.

4

Control any bleeding with gauze compression.

5

Apply antiseptic/poultice and bandage hoof with gauze, Vetrap/Elastikon, and duct tape.

2. **Clean the wound:** The next step is to clean the wound as thoroughly as possible. This can be done using a mild antiseptic solution, such as hydrogen peroxide or betadine, and a sterile gauze pad. Clean the area around the wound to remove any dirt or debris.

3. **Secure or remove foreign objects:** Generally, you should not attempt to remove an object from the hoof if you are unsure of its size or depth of penetration. Large objects, such as long screws, should be secured and padded and only removed by a veterinarian. However, if leaving the object in place is likely to cause further insetertion, remove the object while making note of its location and orientation. Small objects, such as thorns or small nails can usually be removed safely, being careful not to create a larger wound.

4. **Control bleeding:** If the wound is bleeding, apply direct pressure to the area using a clean bandage or gauze pad. This will help control the bleeding and prevent further wound contamination.

5. **Apply a dressing:** After the wound has been cleaned and the bleeding controlled, apply a dressing to protect the wound and prevent further contamination. Use a sterile bandage or gauze pad, and secure it in place using Vetrap or adhesive tape.

6. **Keep the horse off the injured limb:** If the horse cannot bear weight on the limb, it is best to keep it confined to a small area.

It is very important to handle the horse with great care and to take the appropriate measures to avoid further injury. Remember that it is always best to consult a veterinarian, as they will be able to give you the best advice on how to treat the wound and how to prevent further complications.

Fracture Treatment

Administering first aid to a horse with a fracture in its hoof or distal limb can be a complex process that requires specialized knowledge and equipment, so it is necessary to contact a veterinarian as soon as possible. Here are the general steps to follow when providing first aid for a fracture:

1 Keep the injured horse still and calm.

2 Call an emeregency veterinarian.

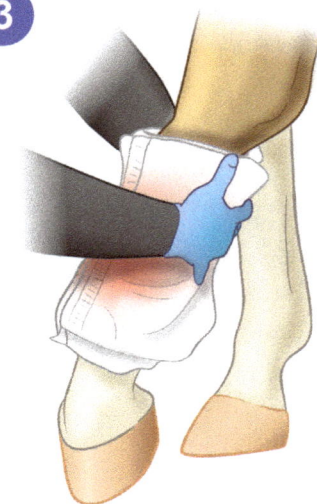

3 Use a clean towel or gauze to reduce any possible bleeding.

1. **Stay with the horse:** Stay with the horse and try to keep him calm. Do not attempt to move the horse. If possible, have another person bring food and water to the horse; this may help keep him from moving around. Bringing another horse to the location may also be calming to the injured horse.

2. **Control bleeding:** If the skin is broken, attempt to control bleeding by compression with gauze, bandages, or clean clothing.

A fracture to a major bone in the horse's limb can be life-threatening and requires veterinary treatment and stabilization as soon as possible. A fracture to the coffin bone can be somewhat stabilized by the hoof capsule itself, however it may be necessary to contact a farrier for supportive shoeing.

Sprain or Soft Tissue Injury

Administering first aid to a horse with a tendon or ligament injury is a complex process that should be done by a veterinarian or professional. However, here are some general steps that can be taken as a horse owner to help your horse before a veterinarian arrives:

1. **Assess the injury:** Observe your horse's behavior and look for signs of injury, such as lameness, swelling, heat, or reluctance to move.

2. **Restrain the horse:** Gently restrain the horse in a safe and secure area to prevent further injury.

3. **Cold therapy:** Apply cold therapy to the injured area using ice packs or cold water to reduce inflammation and pain.

4. **Support bandaging:** Apply bandages to support the injured area, but make sure not to bandage too tightly as this can restrict blood flow.

5. **Keep the horse comfortable:** Provide a comfortable and clean environment for the horse to rest and recover.

6. **Administer pain medication:** If your veterinarian advises it, administer pain medication as directed by your veterinarian.

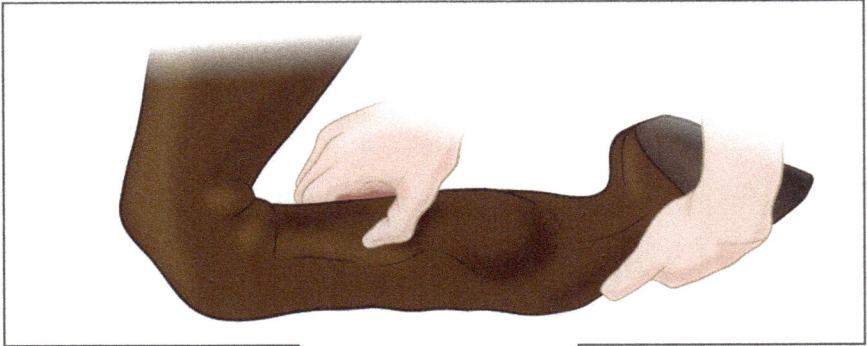

1

Identify injury location

2

Reduce inflammation
with ice or cold hosing

3

Wrap

Head ➡ Tail

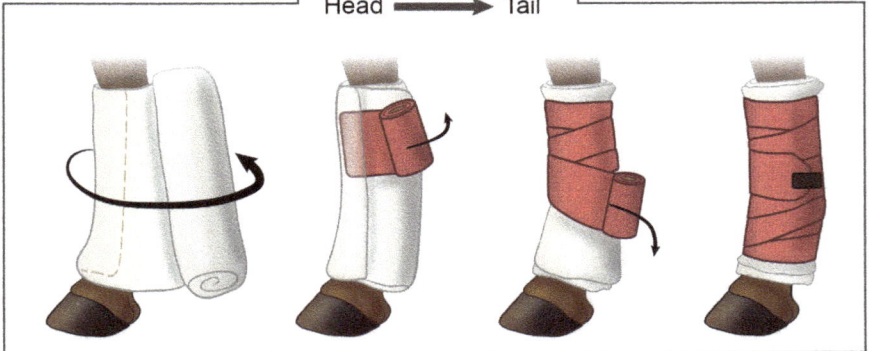

The steps above should be considered as a general guide and the specific steps and treatment will depend on the nature and severity of the injury. Therefore, it is vital to seek professional help as soon as possible for an accurate diagnosis and treatment plan.

When to Call a Vet

There are certain situations where it is crucial to contact a veterinarian immediately. For example, if the horse is showing signs of severe pain or lameness or if the injury or condition is not improving with first aid treatment. Additionally, if the injury or condition is severe, such as a fracture or deep wound, or if it is located in a sensitive area, such as the coronary band or near a joint, it is essential to seek professional veterinary care as soon as possible.

It is also essential to monitor the horse's condition closely after administering first aid and to contact the veterinarian if the horse's condition worsens or if new symptoms appear. A veterinarian can also recommend when to schedule follow-up appointments to ensure proper healing and recovery.

In general, horse owners should always err on the side of caution and contact a veterinarian whenever they have any concerns about their horse's hoof or overall health and well-being. A veterinarian can provide the necessary guidance and treatment to ensure that the horse's condition is appropriately managed and has the best chance of recovery.

Afterword

ROPER HOOF CARE IS ESSENTIAL FOR THE overall well-being of horses. It is a crucial aspect of equine health that many horse owners often overlook or ignore. Hooves are the foundation of a horse's body and bear the weight of the animal's entire body. Without healthy hooves, a horse can suffer from pain, lameness, and other problems affecting its ability to move and perform.

The hooves of a horse are constantly growing and changing. They need regular trimming and shaping to maintain proper hoof shape and function. Farriers are highly trained professionals responsible for caring for a horse's hooves. They perform regular trimming and shoeing to ensure that the hooves are healthy and functioning correctly. They also work closely with horse owners and veterinarians to identify and address any issues that may arise.

One of the main reasons why proper hoof care is essential is that it helps prevent many problems. For example, if hooves are untrimmed and unshod, they can become overgrown and distorted, leading to a host of issues such as laminitis and thrush. These conditions can be excruciating for the horse and lead to permanent damage if left untreated.

Proper nutrition is also essential for maintaining healthy hooves. A diet rich in essential nutrients such as biotin, zinc, and copper can help promote strong, flexible hooves. Additionally, providing your horse with a clean and dry environment can help to prevent problems such as thrush and white line disease.

Regular exercise and turnout are also crucial for maintaining healthy hooves. When a horse is kept in a stall for long periods, its feet can become dry and brittle, leading to many problems. Regular exercise and turnout can help to keep hooves healthy and strong by promoting blood flow and stimulating growth.

As a horse owner, you are responsible for taking an active role in your horse's hoof care. This means working closely with a farrier and staying informed about the latest hoof care practices and technologies. It also means regularly cleaning and inspecting your horse's hooves and providing them with the proper nutrition, exercise, and environment.

By taking the time to care for your horse's hooves properly, you can help to ensure that your horse is healthy, happy, and able to move and perform to the best of its abilities. So please, take the time to invest in your horse's hoof care; it will pay off in the long run.

Additional Resources

Some additional resources for horse owners looking to learn more about specific hoof problems include:

- **International/American Association of Professional Farriers (IAPF/AAPF):** The IAPF/AAPF is a professional organization for farriers in the United States that provides educational resources, certifications, and a directory of members for horse owners to find qualified farriers. https://professionalfarriers.com

- **American Farrier's Association (AFA):** The AFA is a professional organization for farriers that offers educational resources, certifications, and an online directory of members for horse owners to find qualified farriers. https://americanfarriers.org

- **American Association of Equine Practitioners (AAEP):** This organization provides a wealth of information on various hoof conditions and guidelines for treatment and prevention. https://aaep.org

- **Equine Lameness Prevention Organization (ELPO):** This organization provides resources and education on lameness prevention and management, including information on specific hoof conditions such as laminitis and navicular syndrome. https://www.lamenessprevention.org/

- **International Hoof-Care Summit:** An annual conference for farriers, veterinarians, and horse owners focusing on the latest research, techniques, and products in equine hoof care. https://www.americanfarriers.com/ihcs

- **The Horse:** This website provides a wealth of information on various hoof conditions and guidelines for treatment and prevention. https://thehorse.com

- **Merck Veterinary Manual:** This online reference provides information on various equine diseases, including hoof conditions such as laminitis and thrush. https://www.merckvetmanual.com

- **Equine Science Society:** A professional organization for equine scientists and educators that offers a wide range of resources, including research articles, educational materials, and a directory of members. They also produce the *Journal of Equine Veterinary Science*. https://www.equinescience.org

- **The Horse's Hoof Magazine:** A magazine that focuses on the latest research, techniques, and products in equine hoof care, as well as case studies and real-life experiences of horse owners, farriers, and veterinarians. https://www.thehorseshoof.com

- **Equine Podiatry Online:** A website that offers a wide range of information about equine hoof care, including articles, videos, and a forum for horse owners to ask questions and share information. https://www.equinepodiatry.com

- **The Laminitis Site:** This website provides a wealth of information on laminitis, including causes, symptoms, and treatment options. https://www.thelaminitissite.org

- **The Equine Cushing's and Insulin Resistance Group:** A non-profit organization that aims to prevent and treat Cushing's disease and insulin resistance in horses through education, research, and collaboration between horse owners, veterinarians, and farriers. https://www.ecirhorse.org/

It is important to consult with a veterinarian or farrier if you suspect any hoof problem with your horse. These resources can be used as a tool to supplement the knowledge of the professional.

Disclaimer

The information provided in this book is intended for educational purposes only. This book is not intended for use to diagnose or treat any medical condition. Diagnosis or treatment of any medical condition or hoof issue should be performed by your own veterinarian and/or farrier. The publisher and author of this book are not liable for any damages or negative consequences from any treatment, action, application, or preparation to any equine after reading or following the information in this book. References are provided for informational purposes only and do not constitute an endorsement.

Author
ERIK SERVIA

Erik Servia is an Accredited Farrier with the International Association of Professional Farriers and a member of the Equine Lameness Prevention Organization. He runs a busy hoof care practice in Cochise County, Arizona.

www.skyislandhoofcare.com

———

Illustrator
KRISTINA SMITH

Kristina Smith is a highly skilled medical illustrator based in Michigan. As a recent graduate from the Kendall College of Art and Design (KCAD), Kristina has honed her artistic talents and acquired an in-depth understanding of medical illustration, with a particular focus on veterinary and scientific subjects. With a strong passion for both art and science, Kristina's expertise lies in creating dynamic and informative illustrations that bridge the gap between the medical and artistic worlds. She possesses a keen eye for detail, ensuring her work is visually captivating and scientifically accurate.

www.greystoneillustration.com